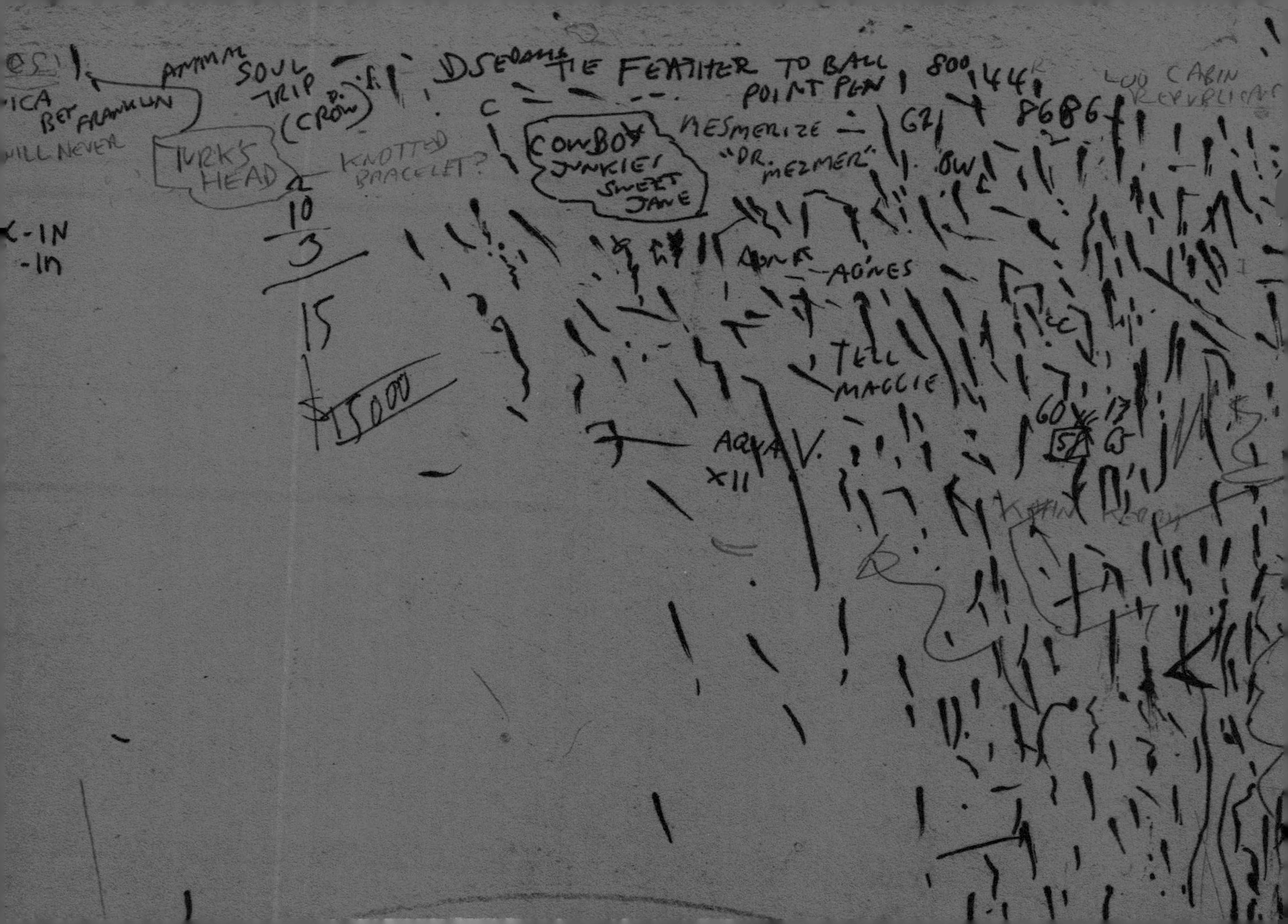

LOG CABIN REVELLING

BETHMLIN SOUL TRIP B. (CROW) DESPERATE FEATHER TO RAIL, 800 144K POINT POW

WILL NEVER

C MESMERIZE — G21 P686f

CONBOY JUNKIE/ SWEET JANE

"DR. MEZMER" OWL

ABNER AGNES

TELL MAGGIE

AQUA V. XII

TUCKS HEAD

KNOTTED BRACELET?

10

3

15

$15000

X-IN
-IN

HORATIO ALGER.

FANTAGRAPHICS BOOKS PRESENTS

500

PORTRAITS

by

Tony Millionaire

Thanks to:

Marc H. Miller, Andrew Leland, Andi Mudd,
William Bryk, Sam Sifton, John Strausbaugh, Joe MacLeod

Most of the work in *500 Portraits*
originally appeared elsewhere, including:

New York Press

The Believer

Baltimore City Paper

New York Magazine

LA Weekly

The Queens Jazz Trail Map

© Flushing Town Hall, 1998

Harlem Renaissance Map

© Ephemera Press, 2001

History Map of Lower Manhattan

© Ephemera Press, 2003

(maps available at www.ephemerapress.com)

and many others.

Fantagraphics Books, Incorporated: 7563 Lake City Way NE. Seattle WA 98115 USA.

Artwork *and* text *by* Tony Millionaire. Edited *by* Eric Reynolds *and* Jacob Covey. Designed *by* Jacob Covey.
Associate Publisher: Eric Reynolds. Publishers: Gary Groth *and* Kim Thompson.

Distributed in the United States by W.W. Norton & Company (800-233-4830)
Distributed in Canada by Canadian Manda Group (416-516-0911)
Distributed in the United Kingdom by Turnaround Services (44 (0)20 8829-3002)
Distributed to the comics market by Diamond Comic Distributors (800-452-6642)

First printing: October 2011. ISBN 978-1-60699-473-3. Printed in Singapore.

A FANTAGRAPHICS BOOK

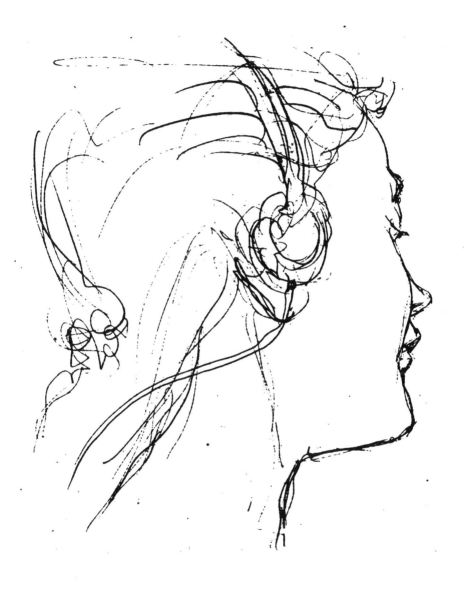

For Becky.

:𝔐: y grandfather Page Trotter was an illustrator; during the Depression he drew roses for a greeting card company. My mother says she remembers how terrible she felt when she was 8 years old, watching him draw and color a perfect rose, and she accidentally knocked an ink bottle onto his drawing. The ink ran down his drafting table, ruining the art. I'm including two drawings in the book by my daughters, Pearl and Phoebe.

GRAMPOP

YUKIO MISHIMA.

AYUN HALLIDAY.

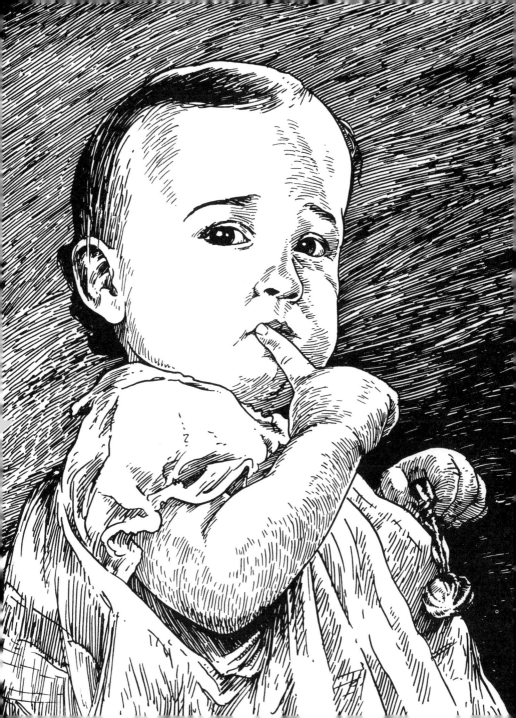

NYC PULBIC LIBRARY LION.

CLEMENTINE BEAN.

BLUE WHALE.

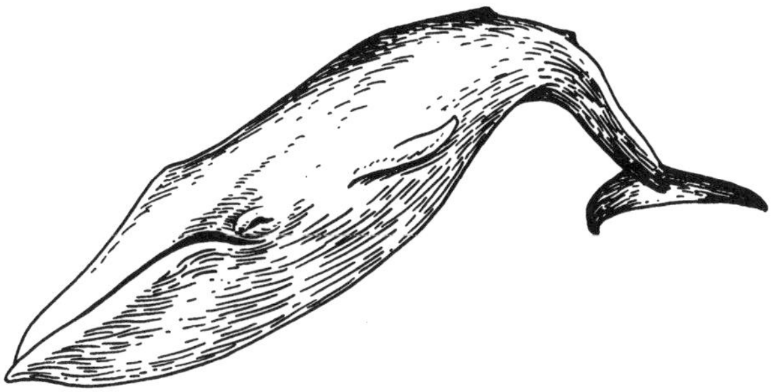

FREYA BLUE.

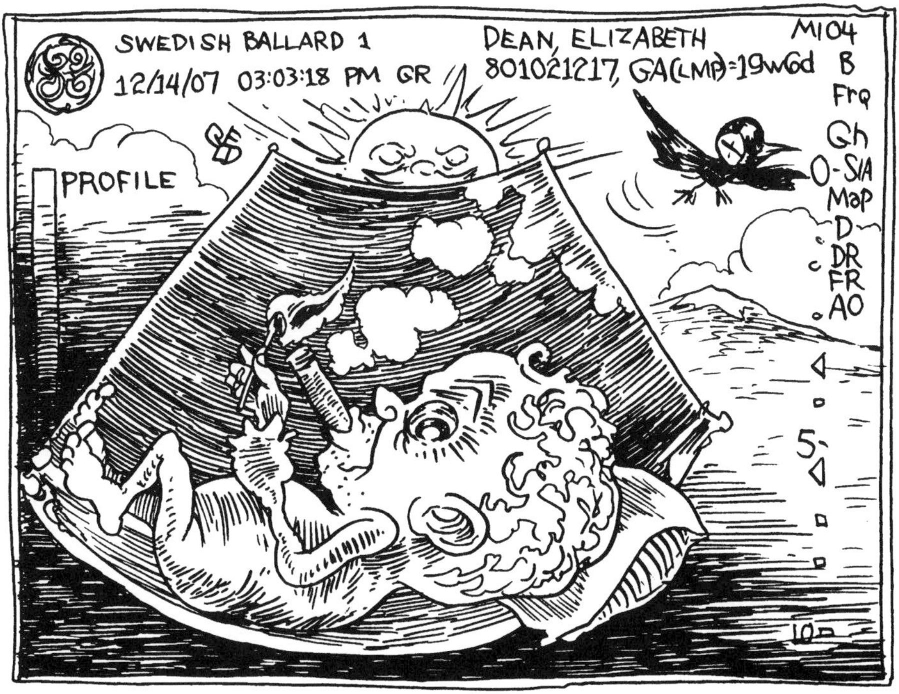
SWEDISH BALLARD 1
12/14/07 03:03:18 PM GR
DEAN, ELIZABETH
801021217, GA(LMP)=19w6d
M104
B
Frq
Gn
O-SIA
Map
D
DR
FR
AO
PROFILE
5
10

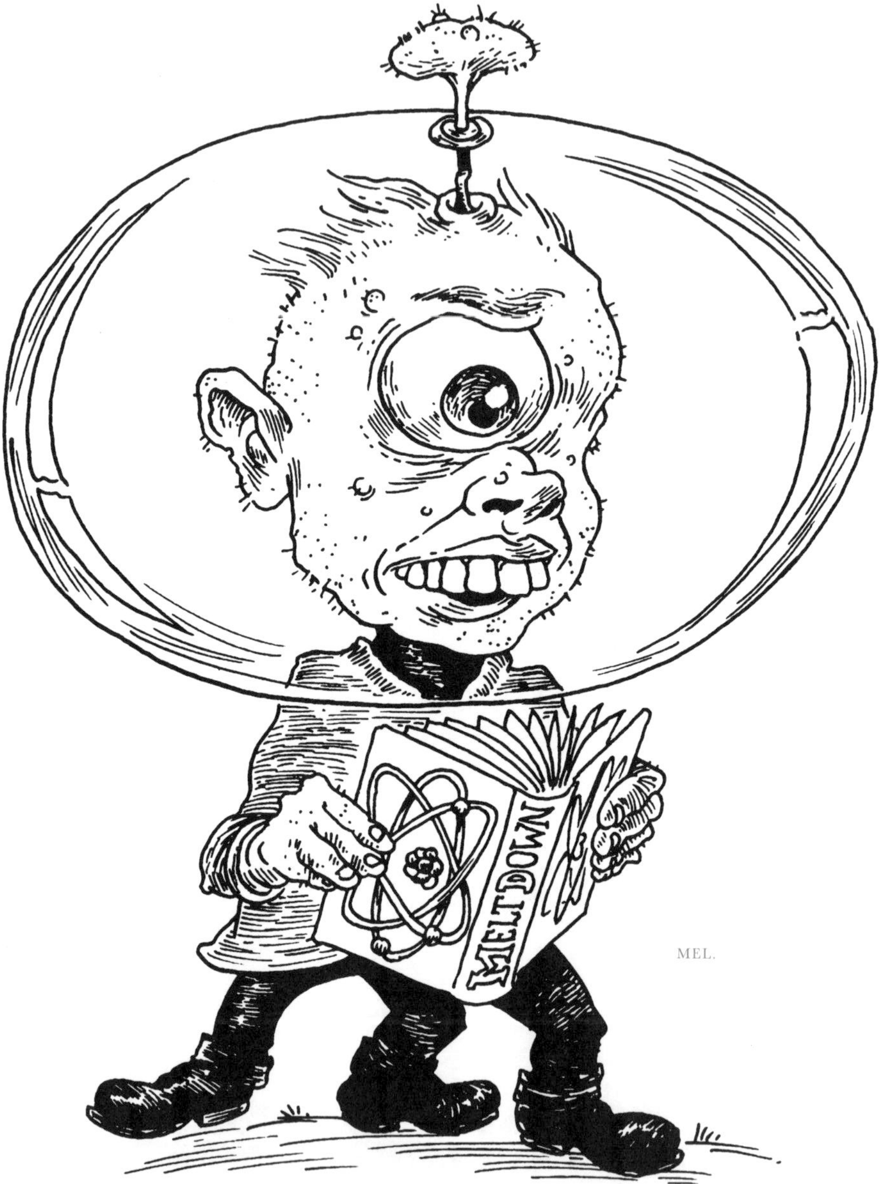
MELTDOWN

MEL.

MAX SCHRECK and
GRETA SCHRÖDER.

JOE LOUIS.

WILLIAM "BILL THE BUTCHER" POOLE.

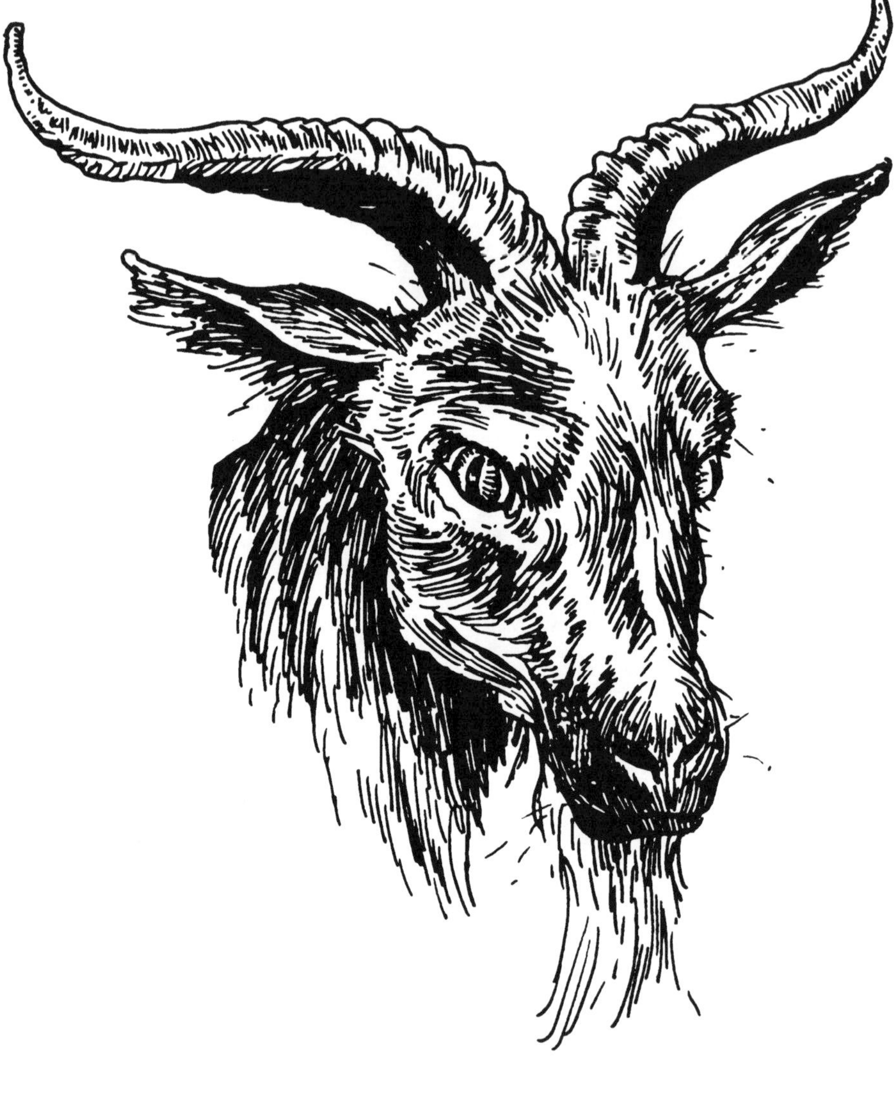

GOAT.

I really started noticing how bogus human beings are when I got to Italy. I lived in Rome for a few months. I had no money and I had to think of a way to earn some. So I drew a scene at the Roman Forum of the ruins. I had a hundred prints of the drawing made at an off-set printing house, then waited by a road on a folding chair till the tourists walked by. I would add some extra pebbles or blades of grass, cracks in the columns, and when Americans came by (here were the big spenders) I would ask if they knew the time. Then I'd show the drawing and ask if they wanted to buy it for ten bucks. That was cheap, so they sold quick. I got enough customers to live for a while, cheaply. I shared an apartment for free with a rich Italian idiot student who needed to learn English. For transportation I took the bus...

ROME   DRAWING

SAM MENDES.

MIKE LEIGH.

LUCIEN CASTAING-TAYLOR.

ALEXANDER PAYNE.

JANE GREER.

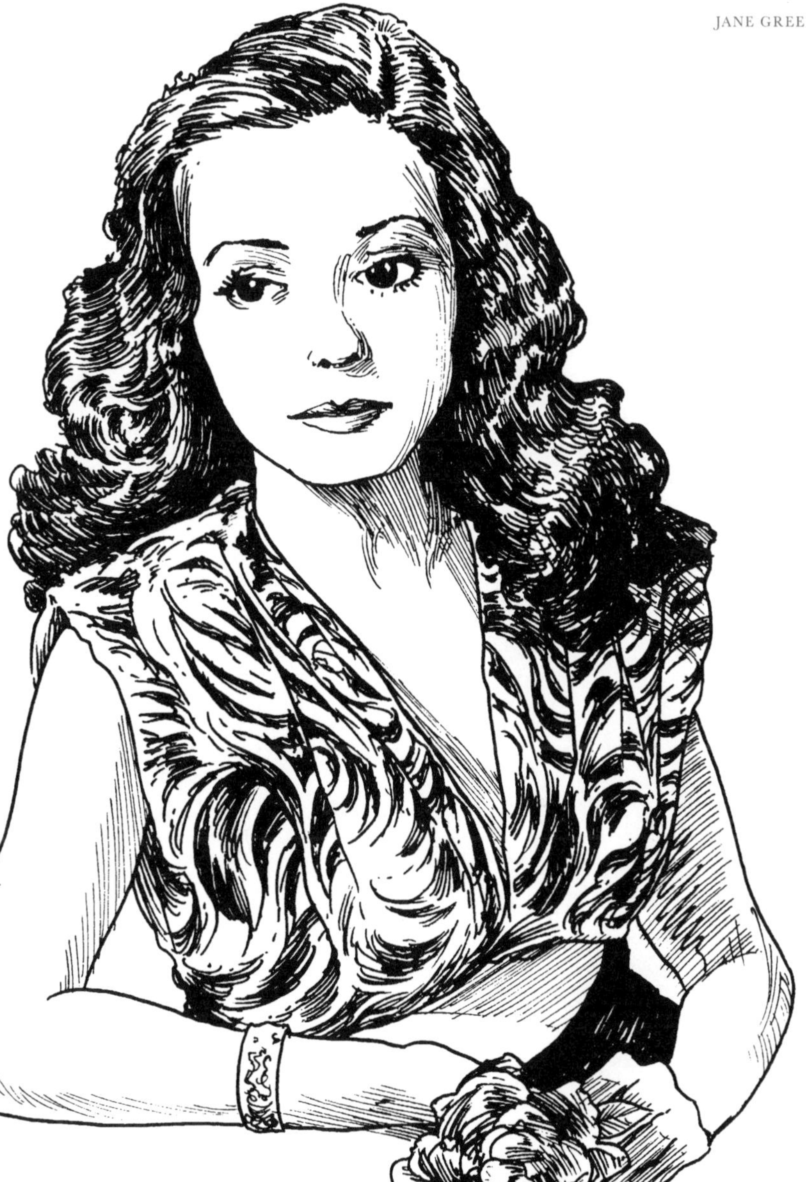

SAMUEL Z. ARKOFF.

GUY PEARCE.

RAY BOLGER.

MICK NAPIER as GOLLUM and NOT.

HENRY FONDA.

PAUL FEIG.

CHARLES GILPIN.

PATTON OSWALT.

LARAINE NEWMAN.

JULIE DELPY.

MARTHA PLIMPTON.

AASIF MANDVI.

THOMAS LENNON.

MICHAEL BELL.

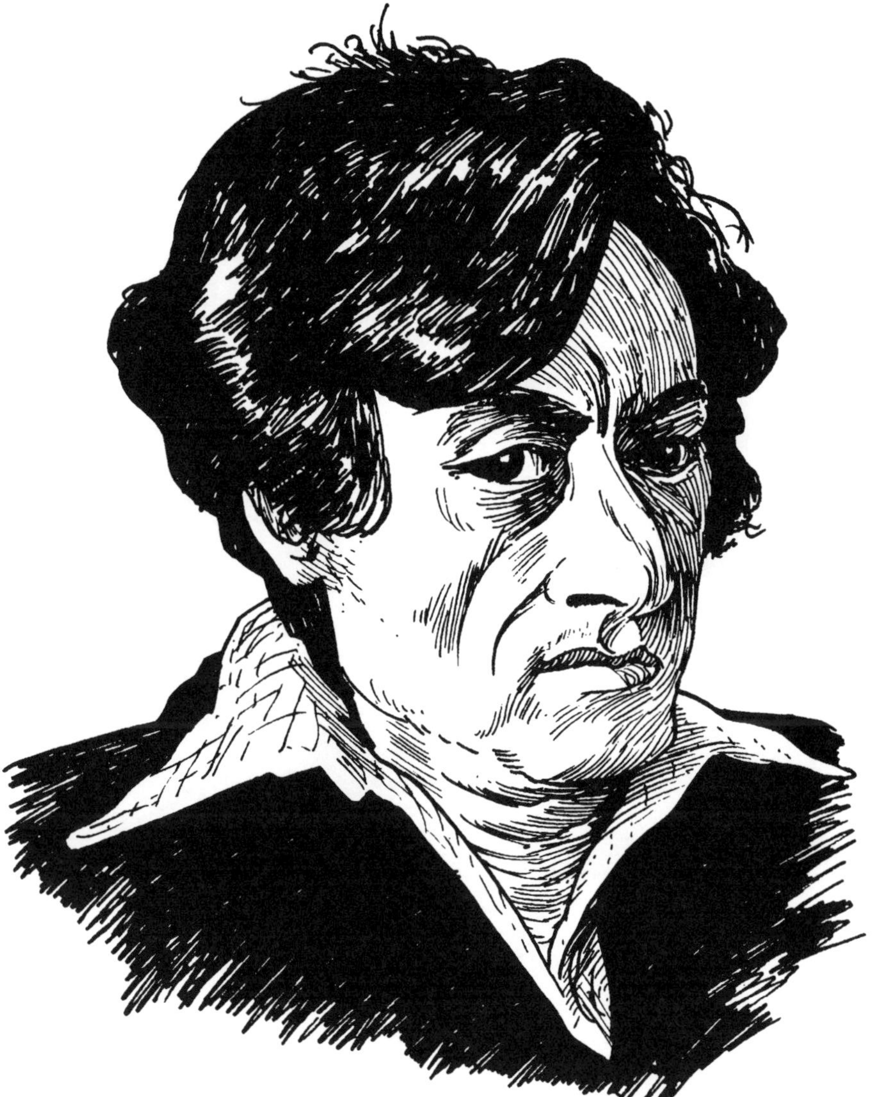

IANNIS XENAKIS.

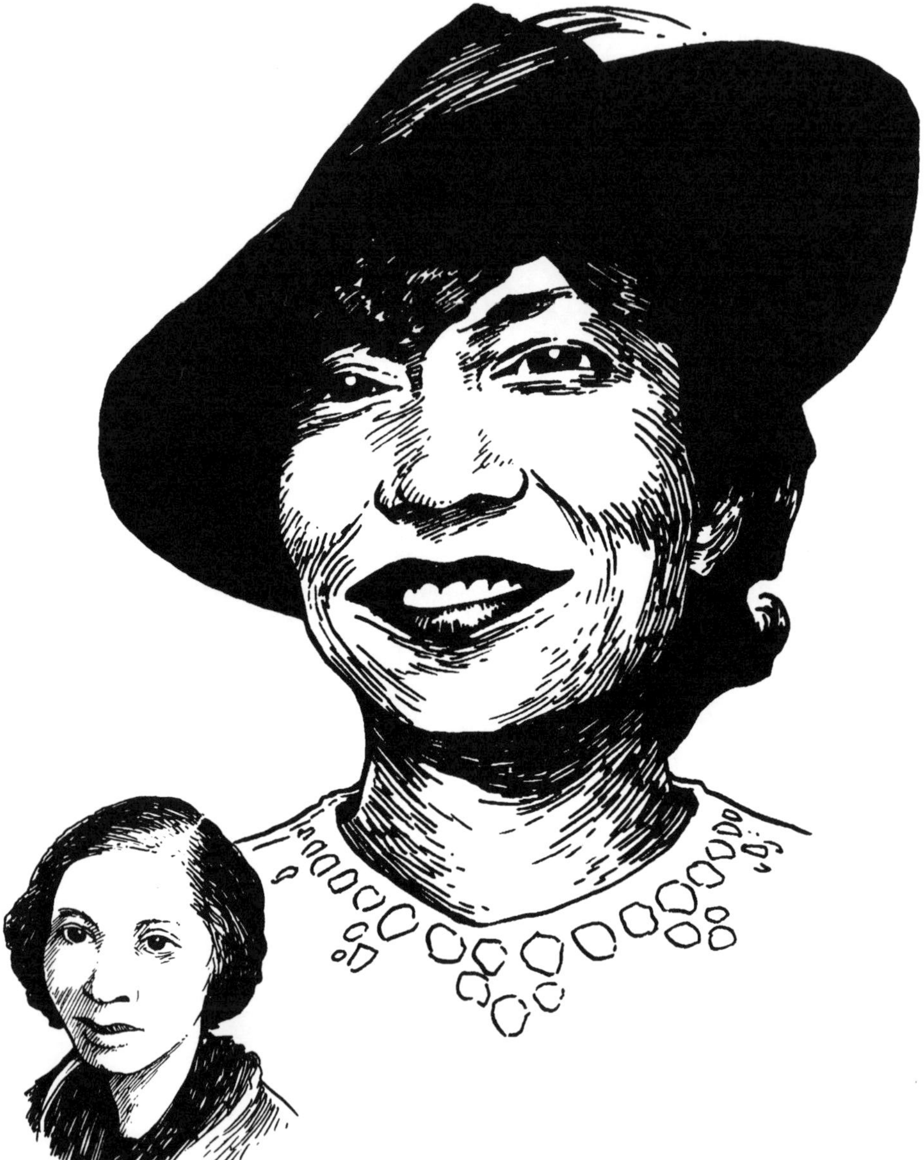

ZORA NEALE HURSTON.

STEPHEN GLASS.

THOMAS McGUANE.

MICHAEL POLLAN.

LANGSTON HUGHES.

NAMWALI SERPELL.

WALLACE THURMAN.

WILL ENO.

JOHN UPDIKE.

TOM BISSEL.

WALTER ABISH.

JERRY STAHL.

WELLS TOWER.

DAVID LEVINE.

DANIEL BAXTER.

HUNTER S. THOMPSON.

STANLEY CRAWFORD.

JAMES BALDWIN.

EILEEN MYLES.

J.P. DONLEAVY.

HARUKI MURAKAMI.

COUNTEE CULLEN.

ANNE GISLESON.

TODD HANSON.

RYAN KNIGHTON.

RICHARD PRICE.　　　LARRY DOYLE.　　　TIBOR FISCHER.

CONFUSED READER.

RAY BRADBURY.

MARIANNE MOORE.

TOM McCARTHY.

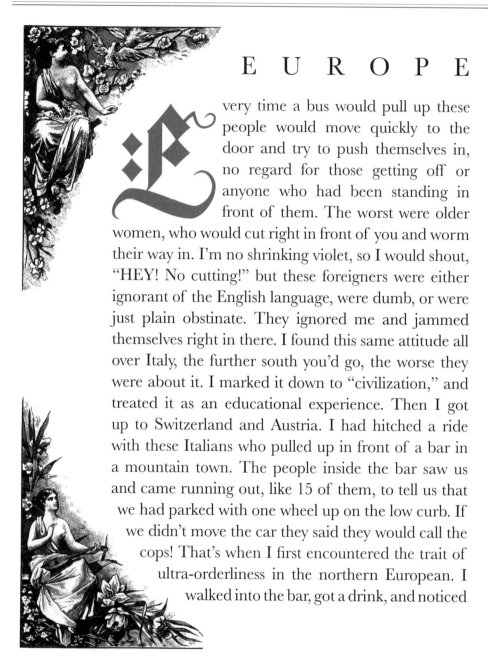

E U R O P E

Every time a bus would pull up these people would move quickly to the door and try to push themselves in, no regard for those getting off or anyone who had been standing in front of them. The worst were older women, who would cut right in front of you and worm their way in. I'm no shrinking violet, so I would shout, "HEY! No cutting!" but these foreigners were either ignorant of the English language, were dumb, or were just plain obstinate. They ignored me and jammed themselves right in there. I found this same attitude all over Italy, the further south you'd go, the worse they were about it. I marked it down to "civilization," and treated it as an educational experience. Then I got up to Switzerland and Austria. I had hitched a ride with these Italians who pulled up in front of a bar in a mountain town. The people inside the bar saw us and came running out, like 15 of them, to tell us that we had parked with one wheel up on the low curb. If we didn't move the car they said they would call the cops! That's when I first encountered the trait of ultra-orderliness in the northern European. I walked into the bar, got a drink, and noticed a bell hanging over the bar. It was beautiful ornate brass work, a nice bell. I decided to test the orderliness of these German-speaking mountain people by pulling the bell to see what it would command them to do. It gave out a loud ring and everyone in the place jumped up with smiles and passed their glasses to the bartender. They all smiled and waved at me, all including the bartender. Of course the bell had commanded them to accept a free drink from me. I downed my schnapps and smiled to all, then headed to the bathroom. There was a small window in there. I squeezed first my bag and then myself through and ran across the meadows! I was having nothing to do with this crowd mentality! Once in Berlin I was standing on a sidewalk, hungover on a Sunday morning. The light was red, but there were no cars in either direction so I walked across. The lady who had been standing

next to me shouted in German, "Ich hopla kambajooku lakke uberlaufen werdeh!" or something. When I got to the other side a hipster was standing there. I asked him what the old lady was saying. "She say she hope you become run over."

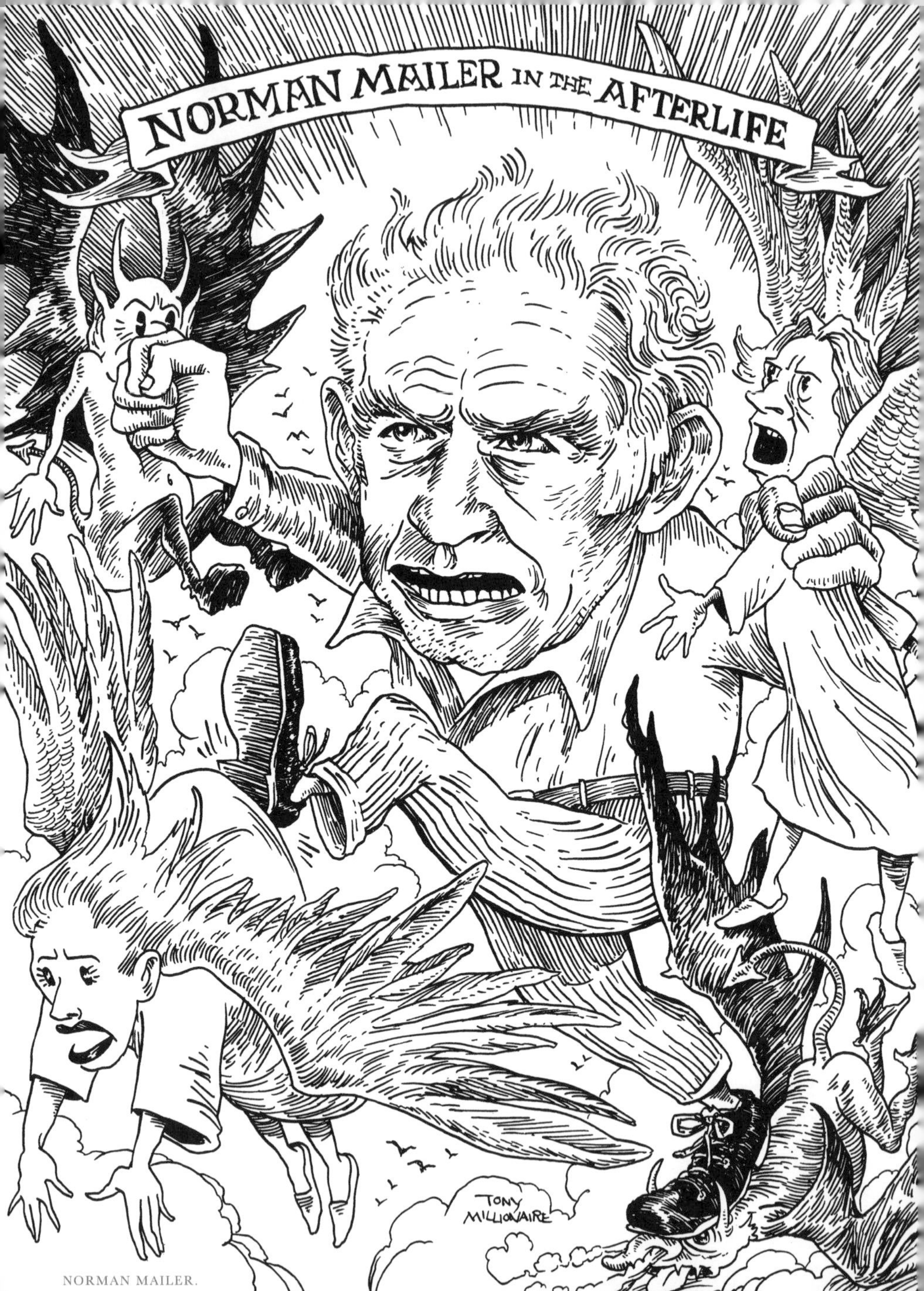
NORMAN MAILER IN THE AFTERLIFE
TONY MILLIONAIRE

NORMAN MAILER.

GEORGE TABORI.

DAVY ROTHBART.

CLAUDE McKAY.

DENNIS COOPER.

EUGENE O'NEILL.

ERNEST HEMINGWAY.

DASHIEL HAMMETT.

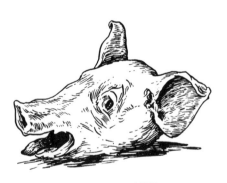

MEAT.

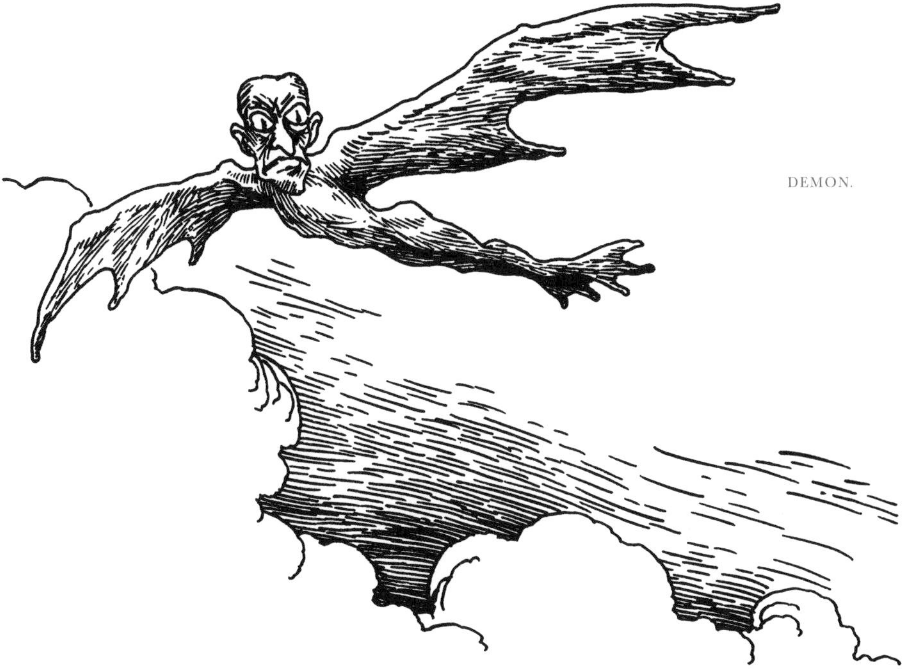

DEMON.

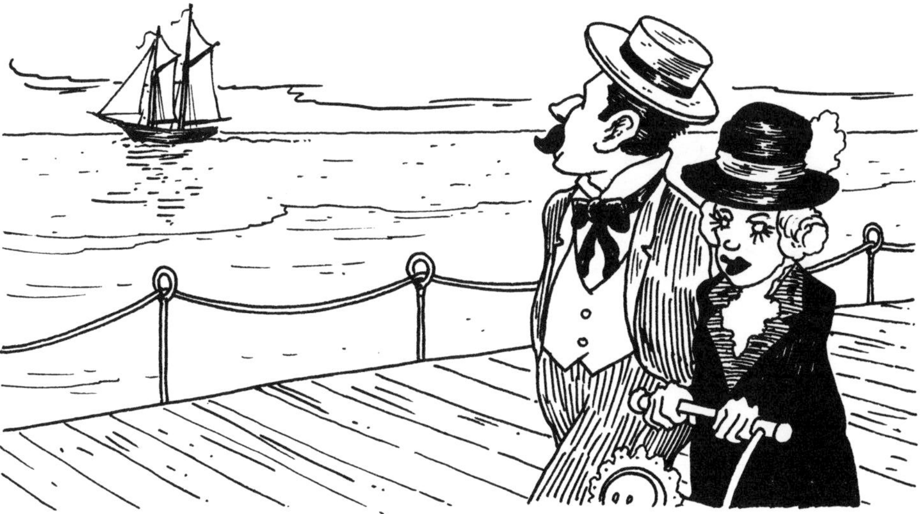

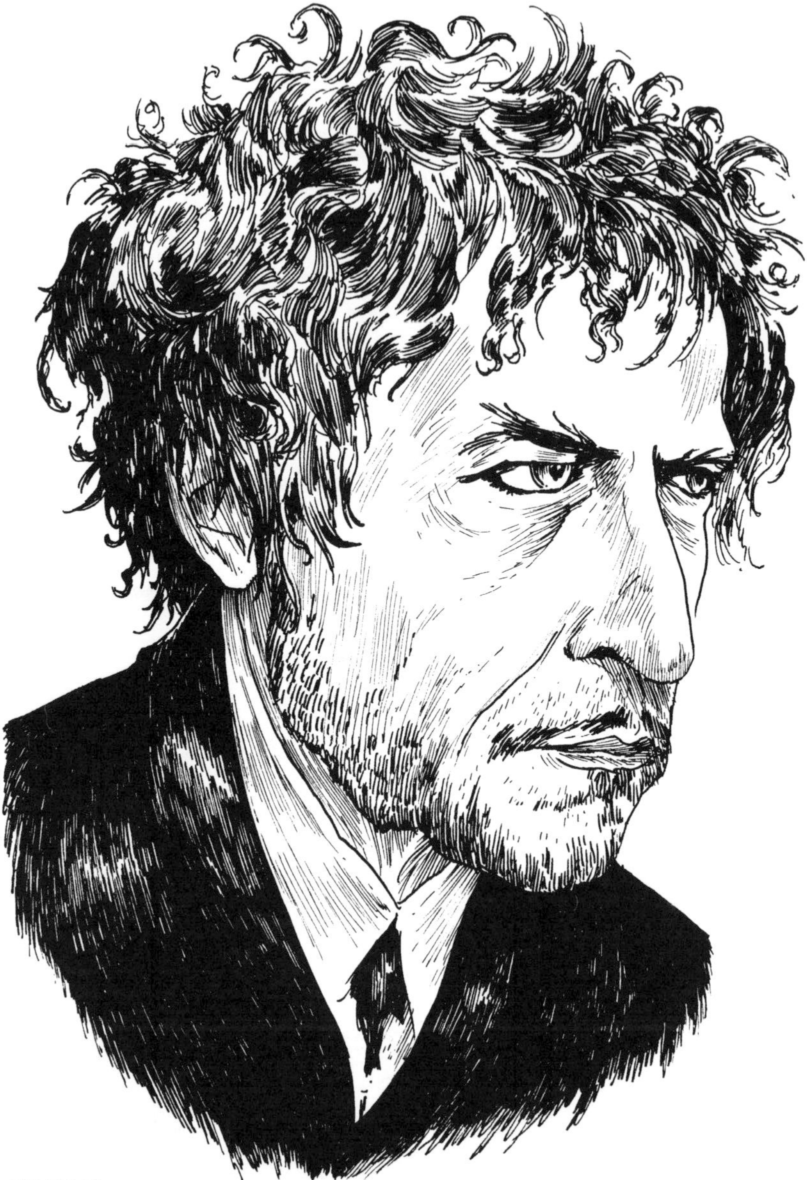

BOB DYLAN.

BILLIE HOLIDAY.

IAN MacKAYE.

LOUIS ARMSTRONG.

LÉON THERAMIN.

JAMES CARR.

JAMES P. JOHNSON.

EUBIE BLAKE, FLOURNEY MILLER, NOBLE SISSLE, and AUBREY LYLES.

BOB MOULD.

JENNY LIND.

IRMA THOMAS.

JOHN RODERICK.

JOLIE HOLLAND.

DAMON ALBARN.

KHAELA MARICICH.

SANANDA MAITREYA.

KEVIN BARNES.

MATMOS.

PAUL SIMONON.

DAVID GATES.

ANDRÉS SEGOVIA.

JOANNA NEWSOM.

JEANNE LORIOD.

QUINTRON.

DANIELSON.

COLIN MELOY.

SISTER ROSETTA THARPE.

FLECHER HENDERSON.

ELLA FITZGERALD.

FRED NEIL.

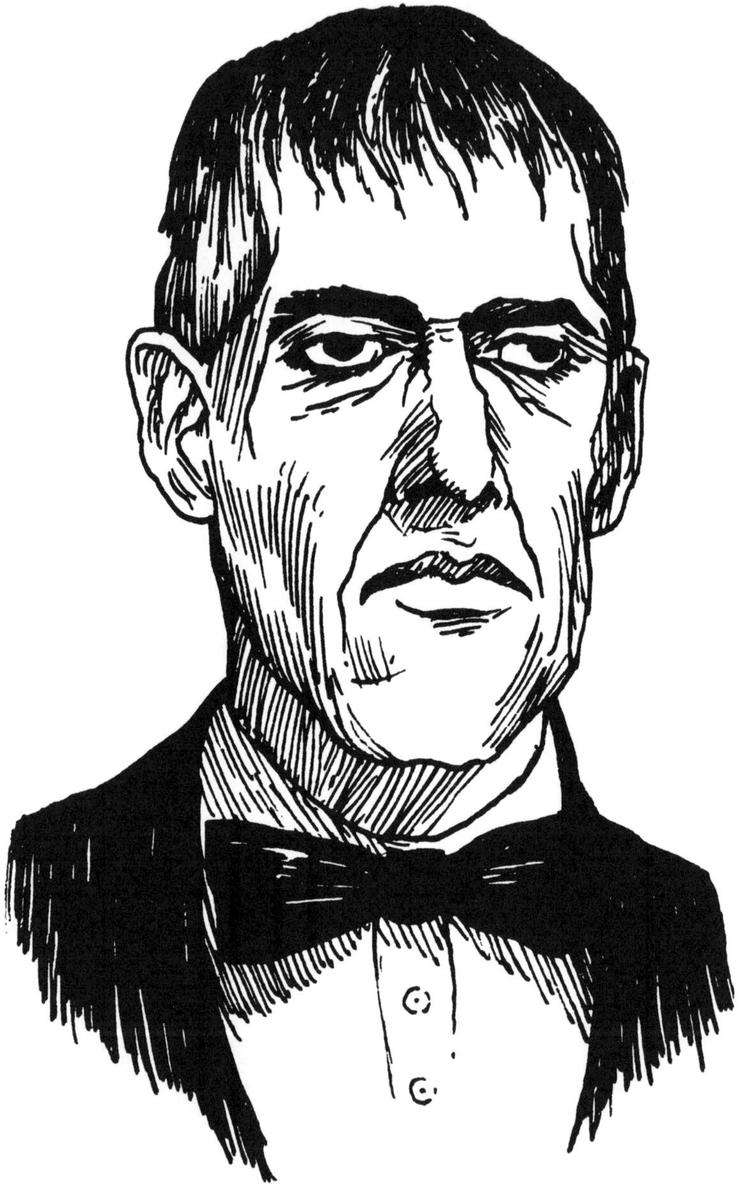

TED CASSIDY.

8 5 %

I t was at this point that I came to a liberating understanding. 85% of all humans, no matter where you are, are bogus. It doesn't matter if you're in Texas or Gloucester, Rome or the North Pole, count the people and you will always come to approximately 85%. So moving to Sweden or Portland because the people are "nice" is a futile move. You might actually get the number down to 70% at first, but eventually you will notice the trait about them that makes them bogus. I lived in a squatted house in Berlin once, you couldn't find a nicer group of people anywhere, friendly, generous, warm, loving people. Squatters in Berlin (before the wall came down) were separate from the normal German population, they were a mixed bag of draft-dodgers, artists, socialists, etc. So one day they had a meeting. They blathered on in their absurd cackling language and soon I realized they were talking about me. One of them, a lovely blonde woman of 25, turned to me and asked, "Tony, do you know what day the trash goes out on the street?" I did not, so I guessed, "Wednesday?" They had a vote right there and kicked me out of the squat. The vote was 80% to 20%. See, they were five percent less bogus than your average human being.

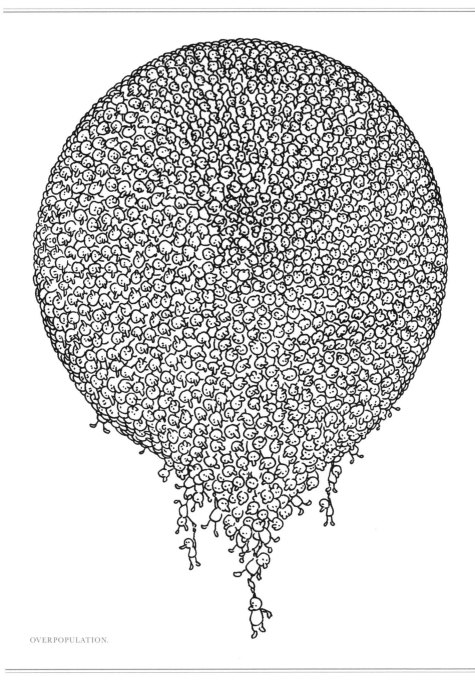

OVERPOPULATION.

LEGGY SUE.

RON ZIMMERMAN.

PIRATE.

POPEYE.

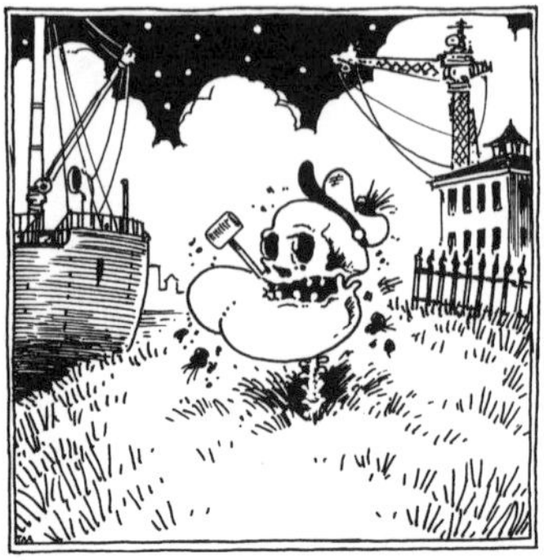

DR. HEINRICH "ROSA" DUBEL.

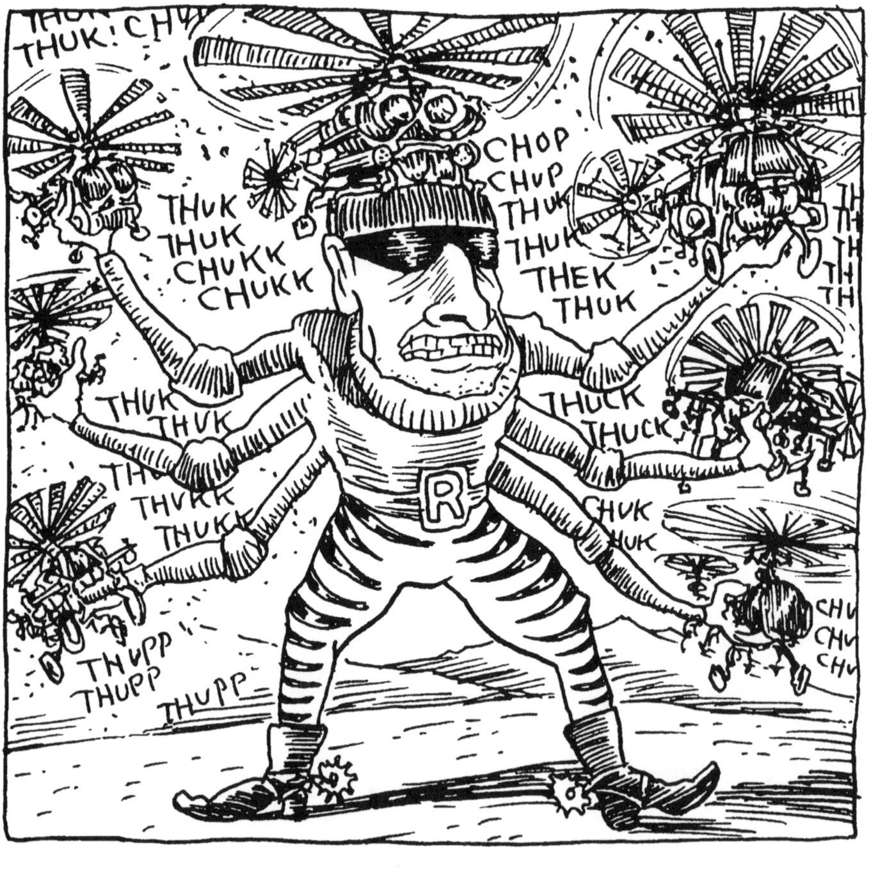
THUK THUK CHUKK CHUKK
CHOP CHUP
THUK THUK
THEK THUK
THUK THUK
THUCK THUCK
THUKK THUKK
THUPP THUPP THUPP

KAZ.

MILLIONAIRE.

FATHER! IT IS I, YOUR SON, BLINKY CROW, IN NEED OF NURTURE!

BLINKY CROW.

MISS PHOEBE BIRD.

DANNY HELLMAN.

HELENA HARVILICZ
and CHRISTINE SHIELDS.

TONY MILLIONAIRE.

UNCLE GABBY.

RHEA PATTON
and ERIC REYNOLDS.

KEITH KNIGHT.

JOHNNY RYAN.

TONY MILLIONAIRE.

JAMES KOCHALKA.

CHARLES BURNS.

THOMAS NAST.

HERGÉ and SNOWY.

JERRY MORIARITY.

LOADY McGEE.

CHRIS WARE.

DANIEL CLOWES.

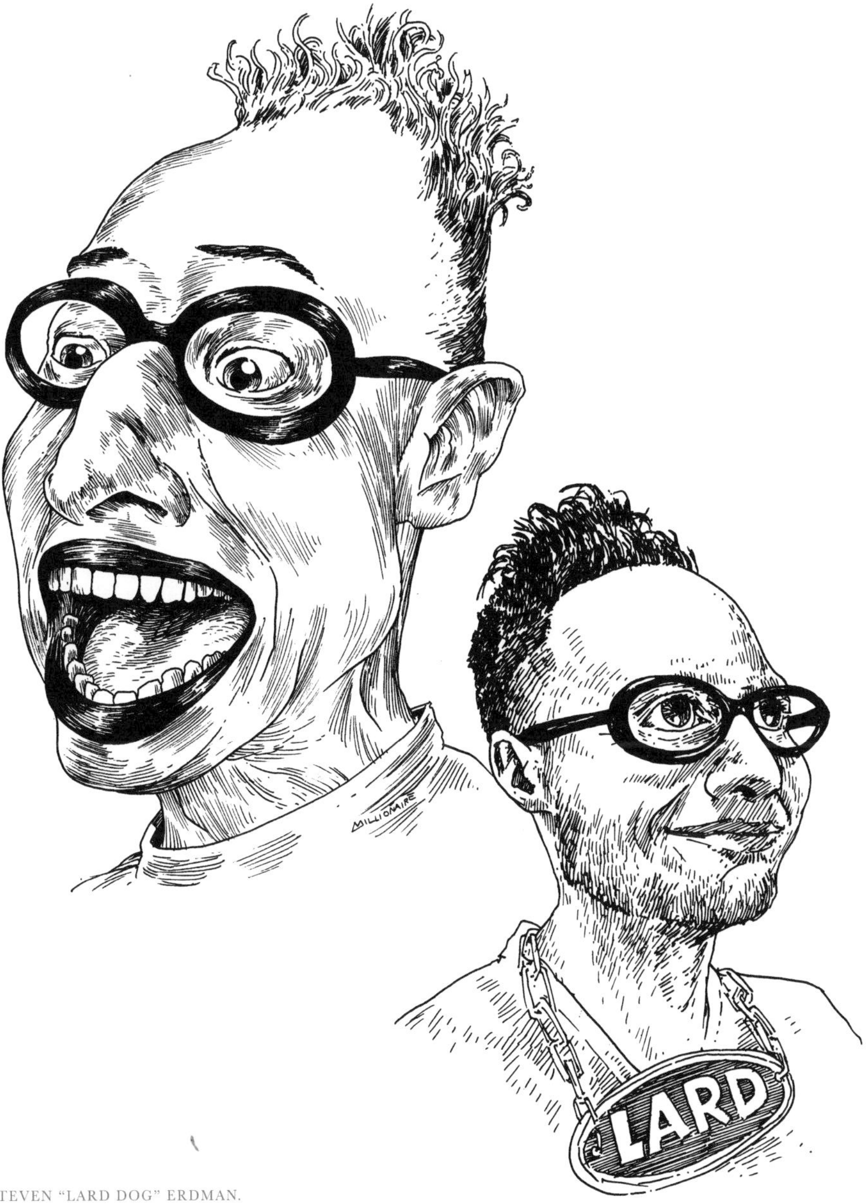
MILLIONAIRE
LARD

STEVEN "LARD DOG" ERDMAN.

TODD BARRY.

EUGENE MIRMAN.

ANDY BOROWITZ.

LEWIS BLACK.

LENNY BRUCE.

BOB SAGET.

SCOTT THOMPSON.

MORGAN MURPHY.

JONATHAN BROWNING, JOE KAPLAN, and DAN WACHTEL.

LYNNDIE ENGLAND.

ANUS-SCOPE.

JAMES JESSE EUROPE.

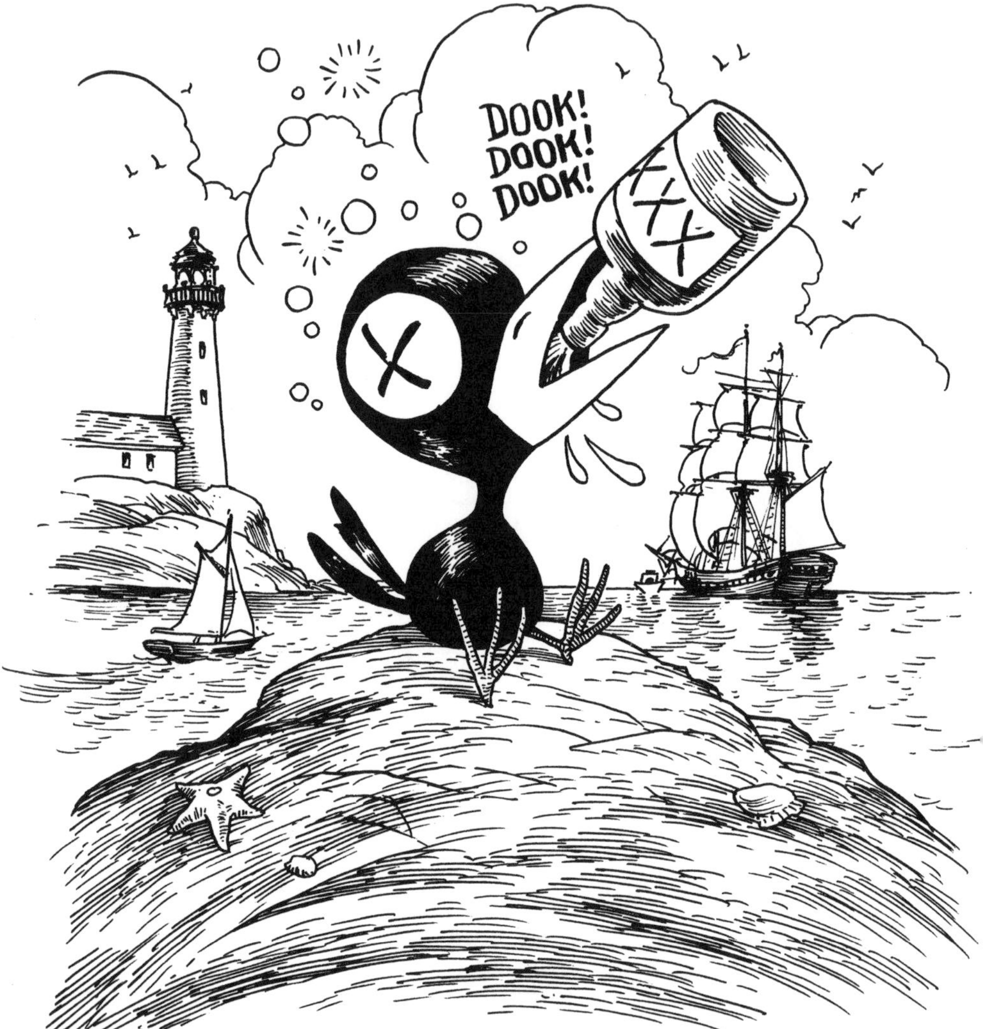
DOOK! DOOK! DOOK!
XXX

DRINKY CROW.

DAN WACHTEL.

IGOR STRAVINSKY.

THE INNER EAR.

PAUL F. TOMPKINS.

MARIA BAMFORD.

PAUL SCHEER.

ANTHONY JESSELNIK.

LEWIS BLACK.

TONY MILLIONAIRE

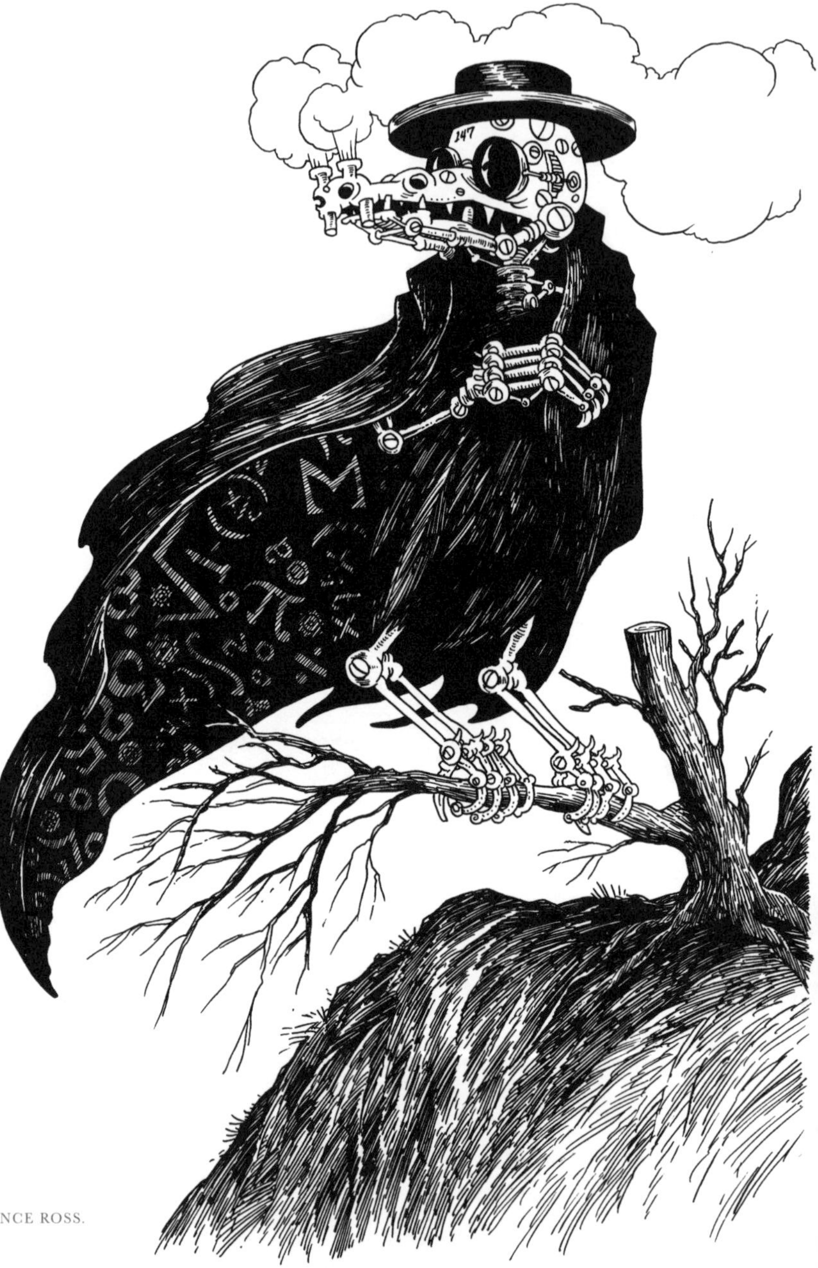
147

DR. TERRENCE ROSS.

GRAND— CENTRAL

hen I eventually moved back to New York I developed "ochlophobia." Except that I wasn't really afraid of crowds, so much as I found them extremely annoying. If you go to Grand Central Station at 5pm you will see an amazing sight. The beautiful hall fills with people, mostly in business attire. They walk through the huge floor, at least a thousand people, not one of them jostling or crashing. This is because it's their daily routine, the rush hour, and they know how to do it quickly and efficiently, like a colony of ants. Of course they are mostly Wall Street brokers and real estate dealers, so they are far more than 85% bogus by nature. Go on a Sunday afternoon at three, it's like the Clown's Asshole Parade, everyone is looking up at the ceiling, checking schedules and maps, rushing in one direction and suddenly turning, or worse, stopping. Everyone is ready for a crash and if you are trying to carry a flat envelope with a freshly inked drawing of a stock broker's house in Great Neck, and you're rushing to catch the last train so you don't have to wait an hour for the next one, you do not want to be crashed into by one of these simpletons.

FRANK W. WOOLWORTH.

J.P. MORGAN.

CORNELIUS VANDERBILT.

MADAM C.J. WALKER.

JOHN D. ROCKEFELLER.

THE BIG BAD WOLF.

SAM WALTON.

A. T. STEWART.

JOSEPH FORCE CRATER.

JAMES WELDON
JOHNSON.

BROTHERHOOD OF
SLEEPING CAR PORTERS.

FREDERICKA
MANDELBAUM.

PETER STUYVESANT.

GIUSEPPE PETROSINO.

PAPPY MEANS.

WILLIAM RANDOLPH HEARST.

CHARLES E. CHAPIN.

NOBODY.

JABBERWOCKY.

PERCY MORNINGSTIR.

HORACE GREELEY.

THE
EMPLOYEES
OF
McCRORY'S
125th ST. STORE
ARE ON
STRIKE!

ADAM CLAYTON POWELL, JR.

BERNARD GOETZ.

AL SMITH.

MARIO CUOMO.

AL D'AMATO.

GEORGE PATAKI.

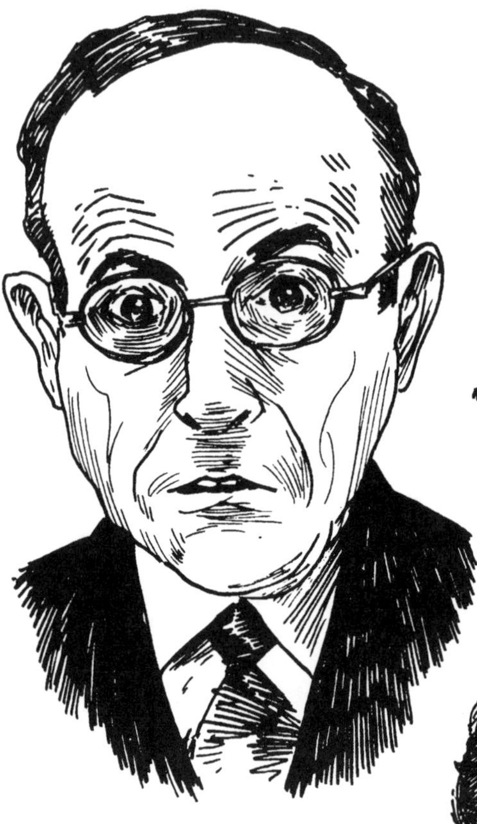

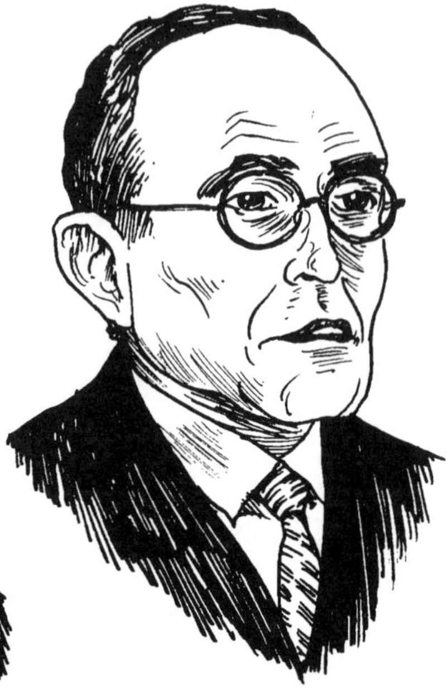

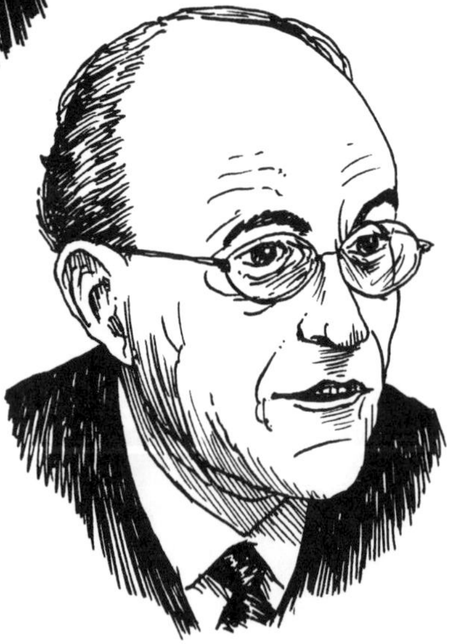

RUDY GIULIANI.

MICHAEL BLOOMBERG.

DAVID DINKINS.

FIORELLO LA GUARDIA.

MYCHAL JUDGE.

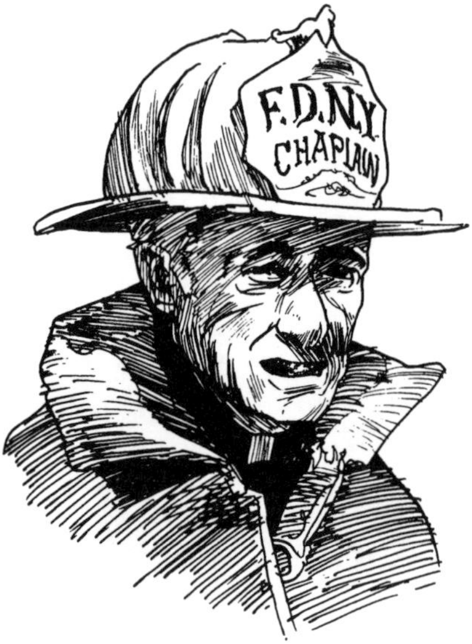
F.D.N.Y.
CHAPLAIN

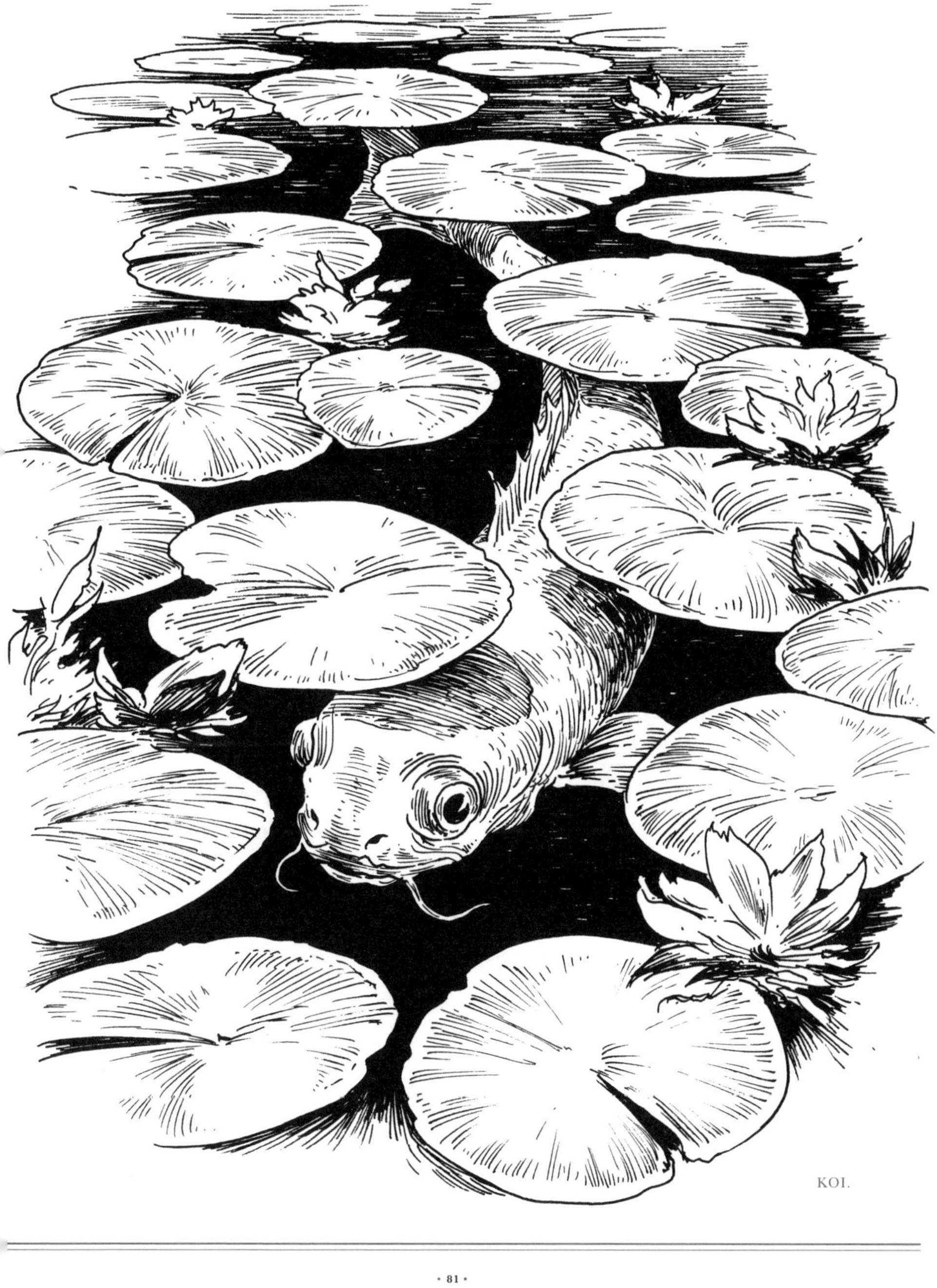

KOI.

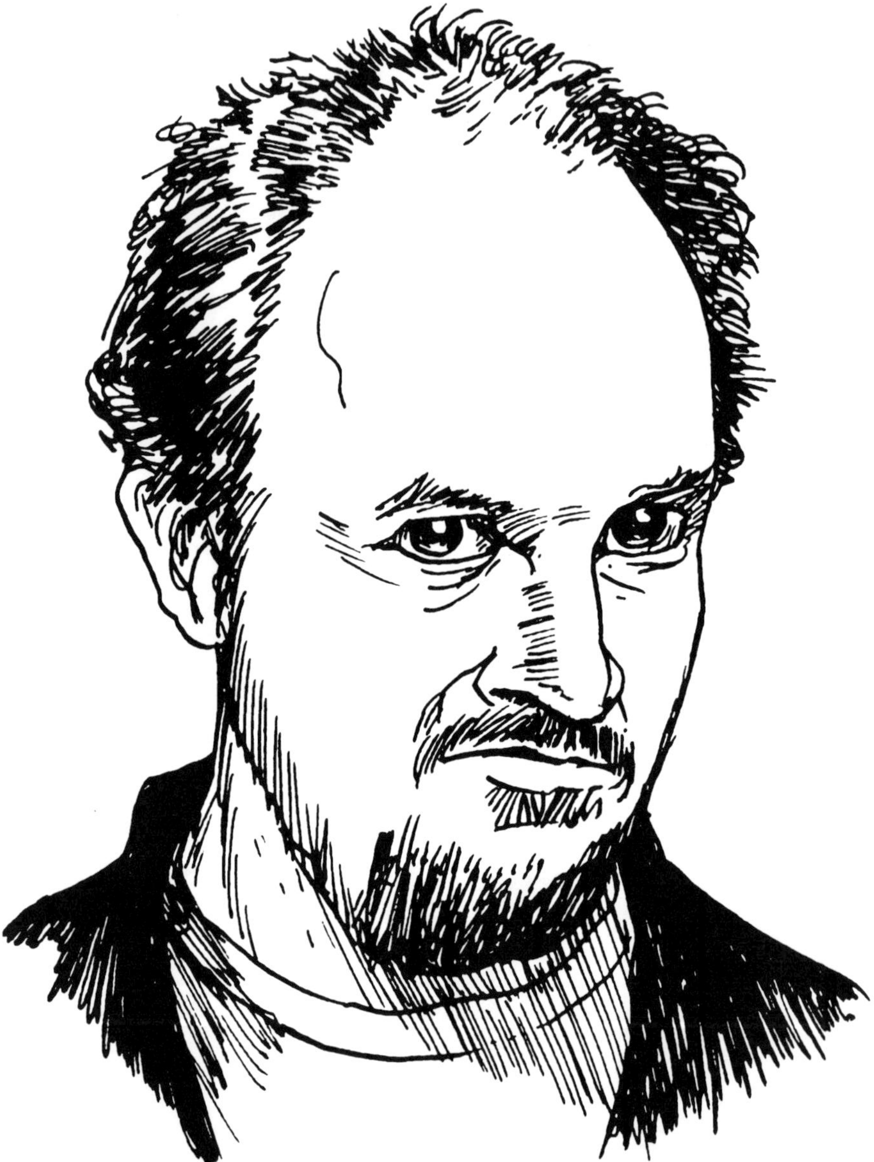

LOUIS C.K.

The sidewalks are another story, much worse. The narrow paths are crowded and someone is constantly jostling you or bumping into you or just stopping in front of you, causing you to crash into them. I would break into bombastic temper tantrums at least once a day because of this. Helena called it "blowing a transformer"—much worse than simply blowing a "gasket." I went to a psychiatrist and he suggested I try an exercise. Start at one end of a busy street and walk the entire length of the sidewalk without ever letting my temper flare a tiny bit, no matter what happens. I tried this and after a few weeks I was cured! As long as I focused on the fact that people are horrible and there's nothing I can do about it, I would never blow another transformer. In those days, however, in order to make a call from the street, you had to use a pay phone. You needed either a phone card or correct change. I blew transformers daily, ripping phones from the box, smashing the cradles, bending the buttons with the receiver. Those God damn phones!

 SIDEWALKS

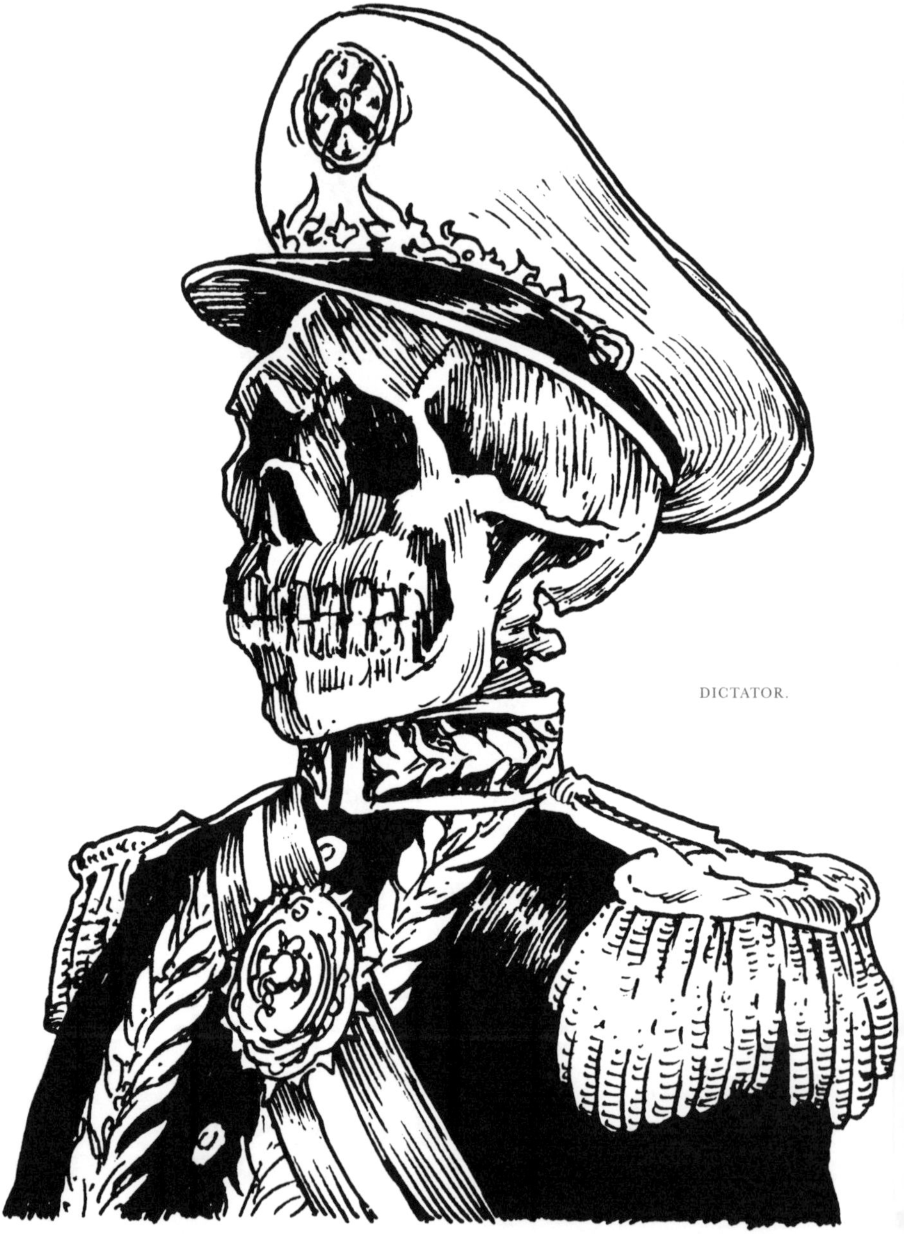

DICTATOR.

GEORGE LINCOLN ROCKWELL'S HATE BUS.

JOSEPH STALIN.

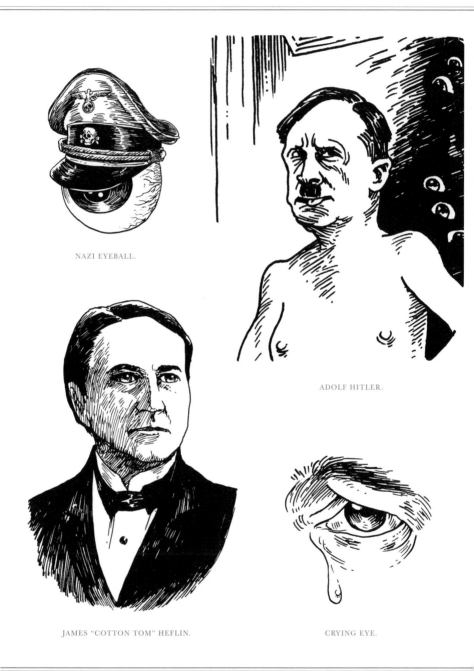

NAZI EYEBALL.

ADOLF HITLER.

JAMES "COTTON TOM" HEFLIN.

CRYING EYE.

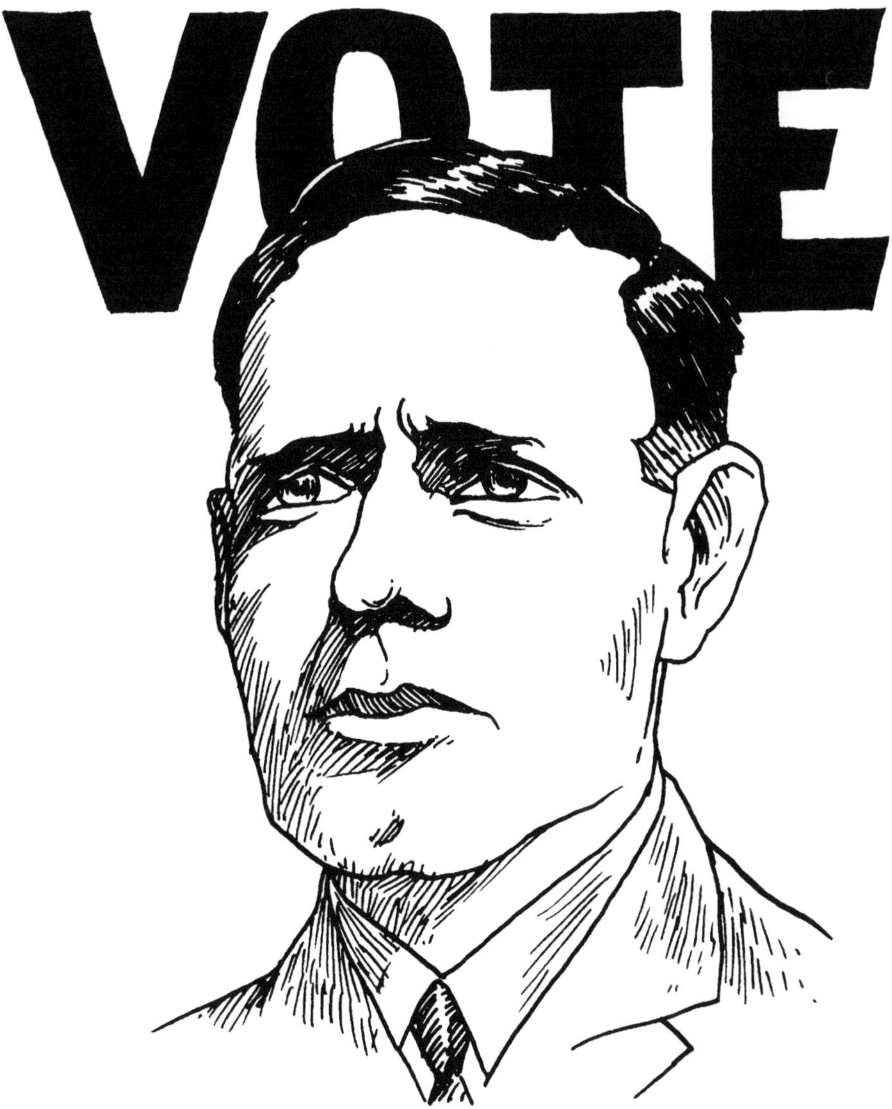
VOTE

CHARLES LINDBERGH.

GILGAMESH.

TOMMY TOPER and PROSTITUE PAM.

EDWARD FERRERO.

HENRY W. HALLECK.

CEREBUS.

ANTONIO LÓPEZ de SANTA ANNA.

ELIZABETH McCAUGHEY.

KING ARTHUR.

TOUSSAINT LOUVERTURE.

MARIANNE CONSTABLE.

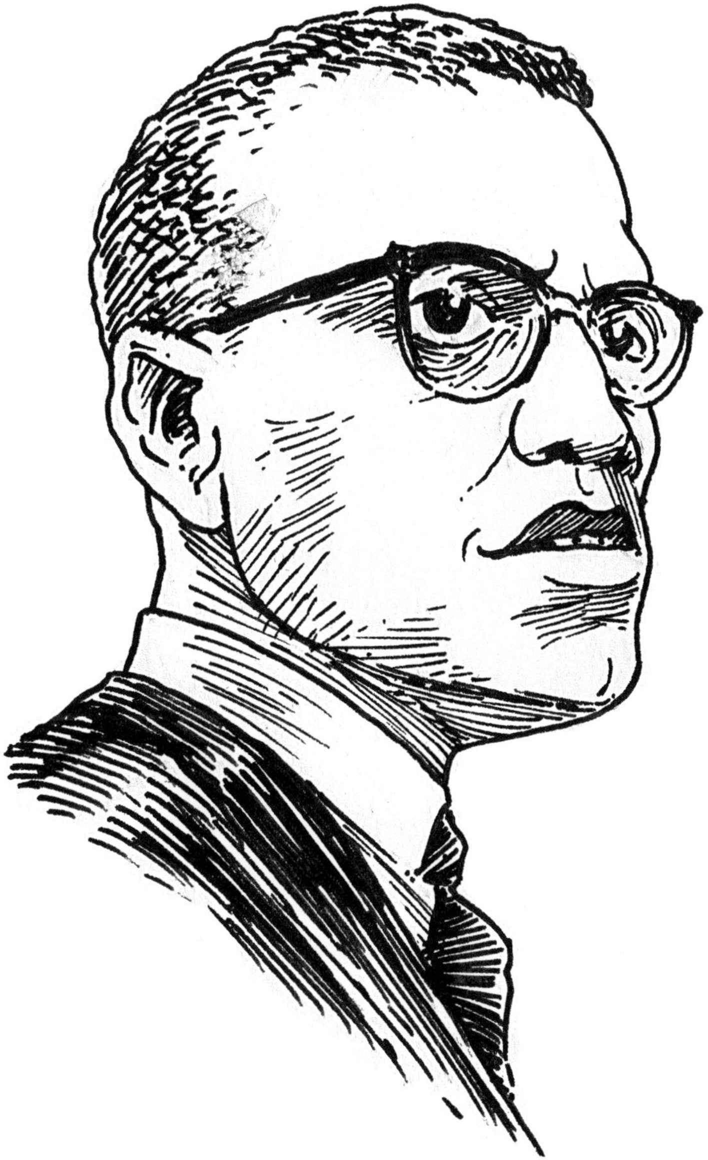

MALCOLM X.

EMMA LAZARUS.

THE HEART.

SUSY SMITH.

SAINT ELIZABETH SETON.

JOHN JAY.

DEWITT CLINTON.

THE MARQUIS de LAFAYETTE.

ALEXANDER HAMILTON.

JIMMY CAYRO.

GEORGE W. BUSH.

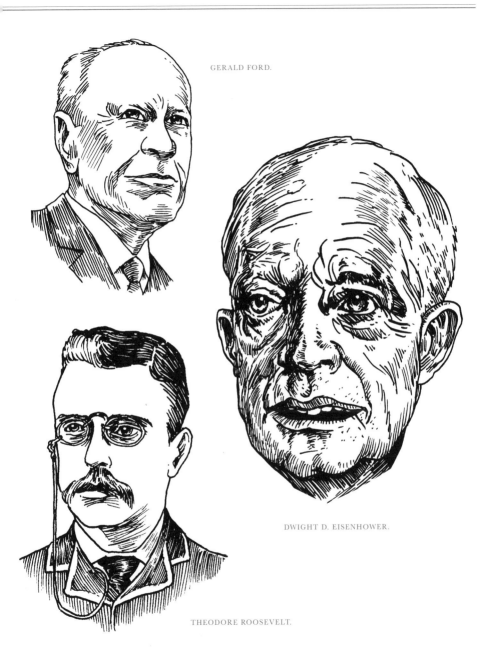

GERALD FORD.

DWIGHT D. EISENHOWER.

THEODORE ROOSEVELT.

BENJAMIN FRANKLIN.

NATHAN HALE.

THOMAS JEFFERSON.

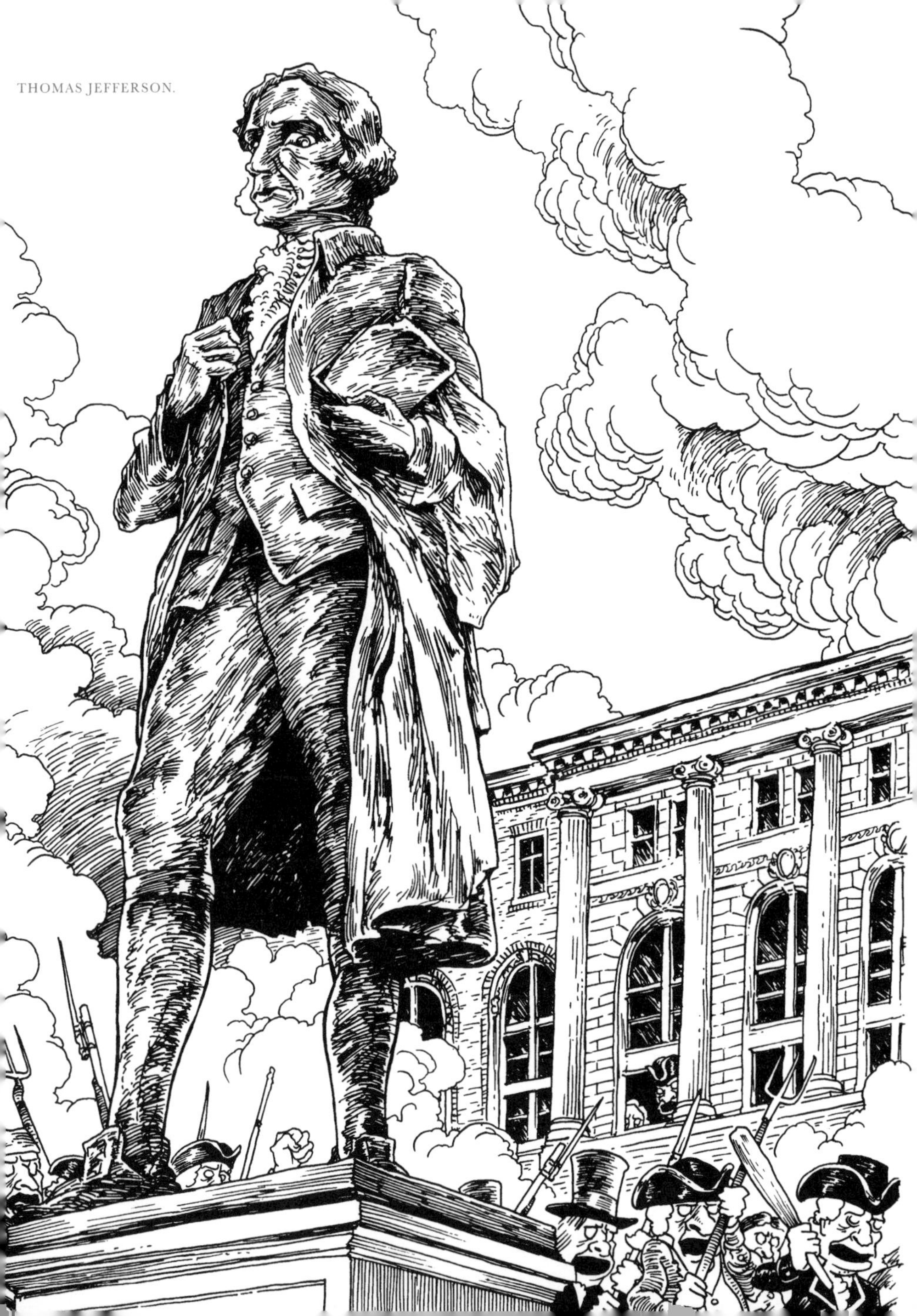

M O B

G o ahead and look through this book, try and find out which of the 500 fit into the category of the 85%, you will find that it adds up, no matter who is counting, if you're really honest. Don't let the famous fool you, they are as not-cool (bogus) as anyone else when it comes to being a person who would tell you your car lights are off at night or if they're on when you park. A Nazi is in here, as is sweet Baby Ayun, the book is quite varied in its selection of human faces. I was fortunate enough to get commissions on jobs over the years drawing some really wonderful people. The musicians I drew were fascinating, there were so many of them, some crazy evil motherfuckers and mostly truly beautiful human beings. I've also drawn many artists, crazy, smiling faces and scowling faces, it doesn't matter, they're probably 85% bogus if you get to know them, the smilers outweighing

RULE

the scowlers. Who knows? That may not be true at all. ¶ Politicians abound in this book, and though it's easy to shout "bogus!" at a politician, it is almost always a misguided shout. Why, if you look through these faces you'll see people who worked very hard to better the world, and some who tried to destroy it. Look at Teddy Roosevelt, in his younger years, glasses on, charging around the world, stomping up San Juan Hill acting like a big jerk, and then saving our National Parks! There are lots of civil rights activists and even guys like Jim Lomako, a neighborhood guy who visits you, very sweaty, and asks you to put a sign in your yard and you do and you will put them up forever because he is such a weirdo and you love him because his biggest platform is stop tearing down all these beautiful Pasadena buildings or putting hi-risers smack in front of them, ruining the view of the mountains! A hero!

A. PHILIP RANDOLPH.

MANASSEH TRIBE MEMBER.

WILLIAM "BOSS" TWEED.

TURTLES.

JIM LOMAKO.

EDUARDO HALFON.

DANIEL ALARCÓN.

SANTIAGO VAQUERA-VÁSQUEZ.

JENNY DAVIDSON.

AMELIE GILETTE.

BRENDON SMALL.

JESSE BALL.

JOHN EHLE.

CLARE ROJAS.

SHEILA HETI.

SUSAN STRAIGHT.

CINTRA WILSON.

DAVE HICKEY.

ADAM CURTIS.

DAVID SIMON.

EVAN CONNELL.

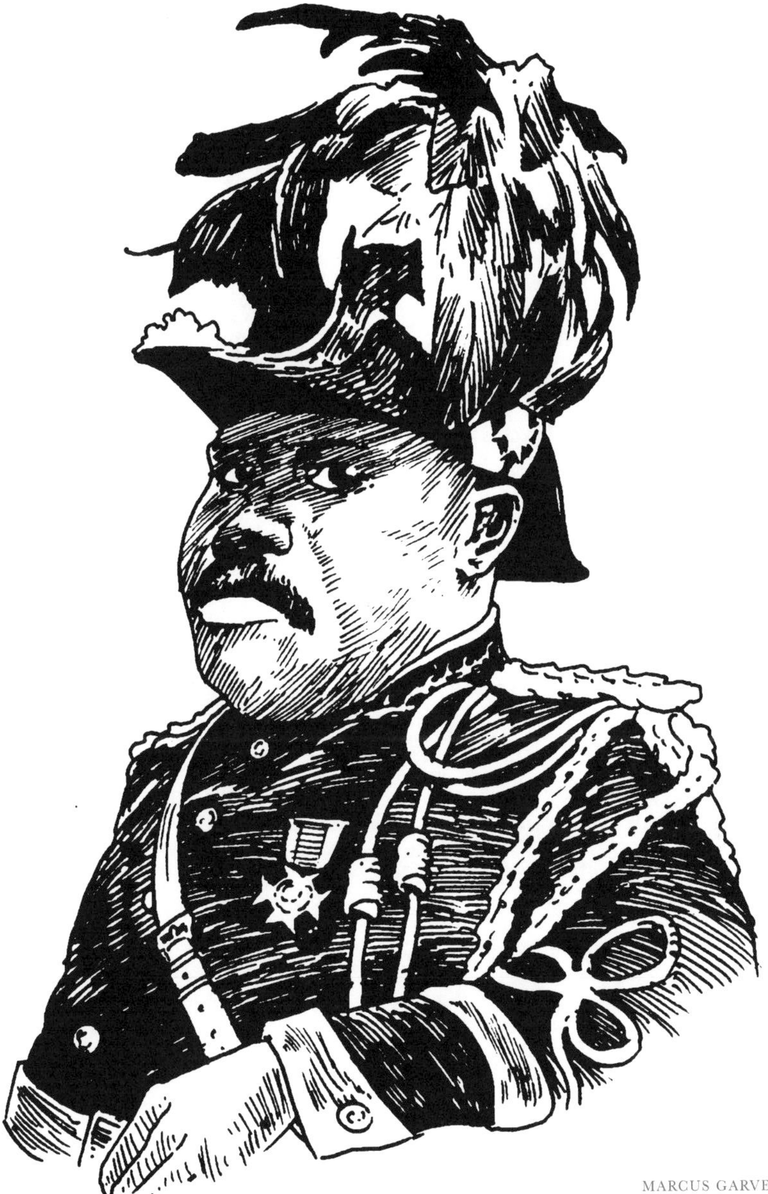

MARCUS GARVEY.

FRANS de WAAL.

BRENDA DUNNE.

MIKE DAVIS.

J. CRAIG VENTER.

RYAN McGINLEY.

WILLIAM EGGLESTON.

MARVIN & MORGAN SMITH.

WILLIE "THE LION" SMITH, THOMAS WRIGHT
"FATS" WALLER, and JELLY ROLL MORTON.

NOBLE SISSLE and EUBIE BLAKE.

W.C. HANDY.

ROY ELDRIDGE.

MARIAN ANDERSON.

CHARLES MINGUS.

BIX BEIDERBECKE.

GLENN MILLER.

LESTER YOUNG.

BEN WEBSTER.

PERCY HEATH.

MERCER ELLINGTON.

PHIL SCHAPP.

EDWARD MacDOWELL.

WOODY HERMAN.

MUSIC HEAD.

RICHARD WAGNER.

COMPOSER.

GEORGE GERSHWIN.

ENNIO MORRICONE.

WILL MARION COOK.

BILLY STRAYHORN.

BOB COLE, JAMES WELDON JOHNSON, and J. ROSAMOND JOHNSON.

MARK VICTOR HENSEN.

DIZZY GILLESPIE.

AIMEE MANN.

MARY LOU WILLIAMS.

ALBERTA HUNTER.

MARK E. SMITH.

THELONIUS MONK.

JOHN DARNIELLE.

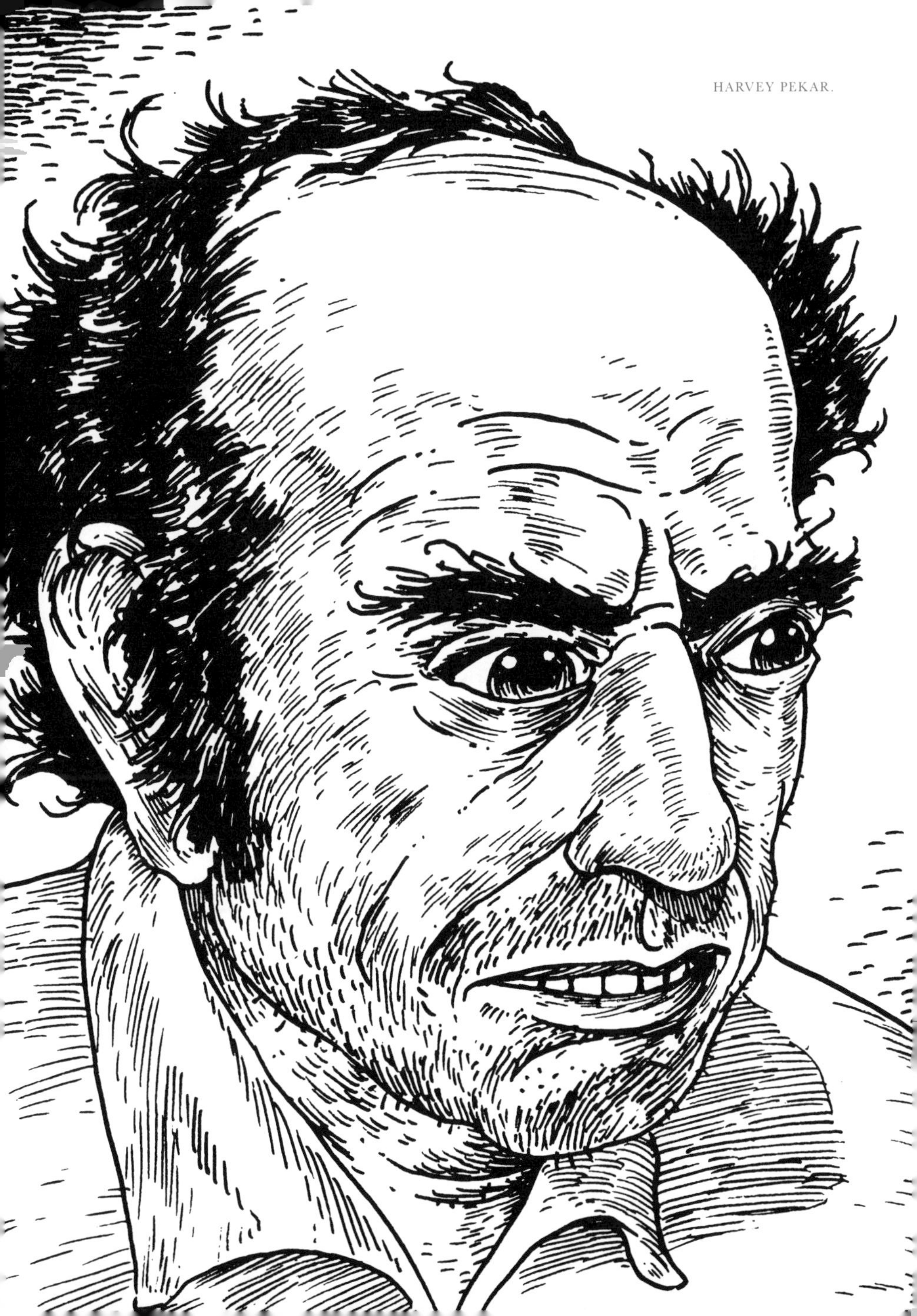

HARVEY PEKAR.

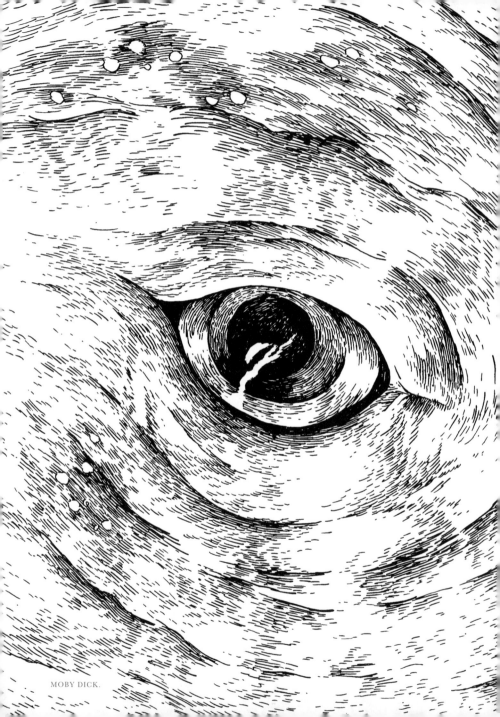

MOBY DICK.

ANIMALS AND INANIMATE OBJECTS

The editors and I have decided to include some animals and even inanimate objects in the book, in order to keep it interesting but also because many of these drawings—Moby Dick, for example—are some of the finest portraits I've ever done. I generally don't apply any kind of percentage grade to animals regarding their qualities as "good people" because it's really tricky and unreliable. The problem is that an animal will turn on you as quick as a human. How many times has a Dad bought his child a chimpanzee only to have the chimp bite the child and the chimp has to "go to the farm." Fortunately for chimp pets, they're really expensive so they can usually be sold to a zoo or a traveling gypsy circus rather than just be sent to the test lab to see if the new Five Blade Fission Razor is bad when it touches the cornea. I don't think I put any chimps in the book, but there is plenty to learn about all the other types of animals.

DUTCHMAN.

JOSEPH "DAGGER JOHN" HUGHES.

MICHAEL & LISA THYRE.

GEORGE W. BUSH
as AGUIRRE.

NACHO.

DON QUIXOTE and SANCHO PANZA.

GIOVANNI
da VERRAZZANO.

HENRY HUDSON.

MATTHEW HENSON.

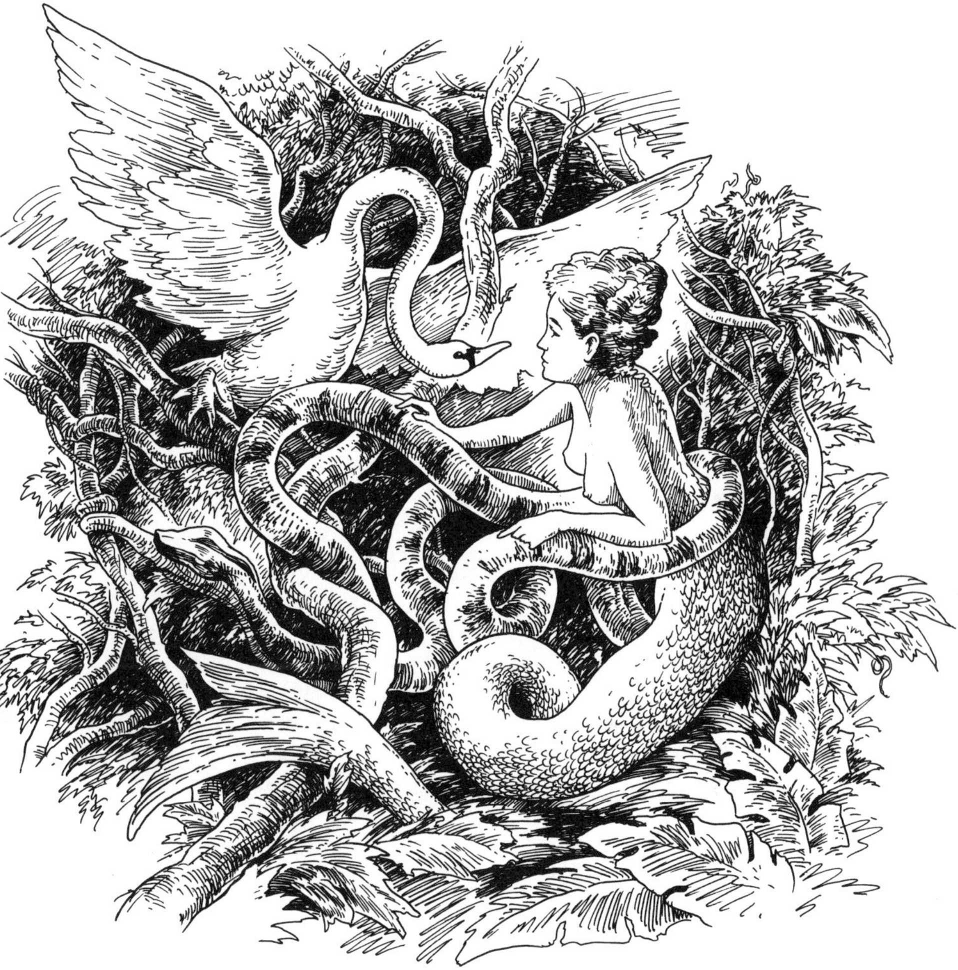

SEDUCTION.

ERROL MORRIS.

WERNER HERZOG.

RINGWRAITH.

TODD HAYNES.

ORSON WELLES.

GUS VAN SANT.

CHARACTER FROM GUY MADDIN FILM.

DON HERTZFELDT.

HARMONY KORINE.

ILISA BARBASH.

MICHAEL ALMEREYDA.

STEVEN SPIELBERG.

JOHN SAYLES.

C.S. LEIGH.

MARK ROMANEK.

DAVID FINCHER.

GUY MADDIN.

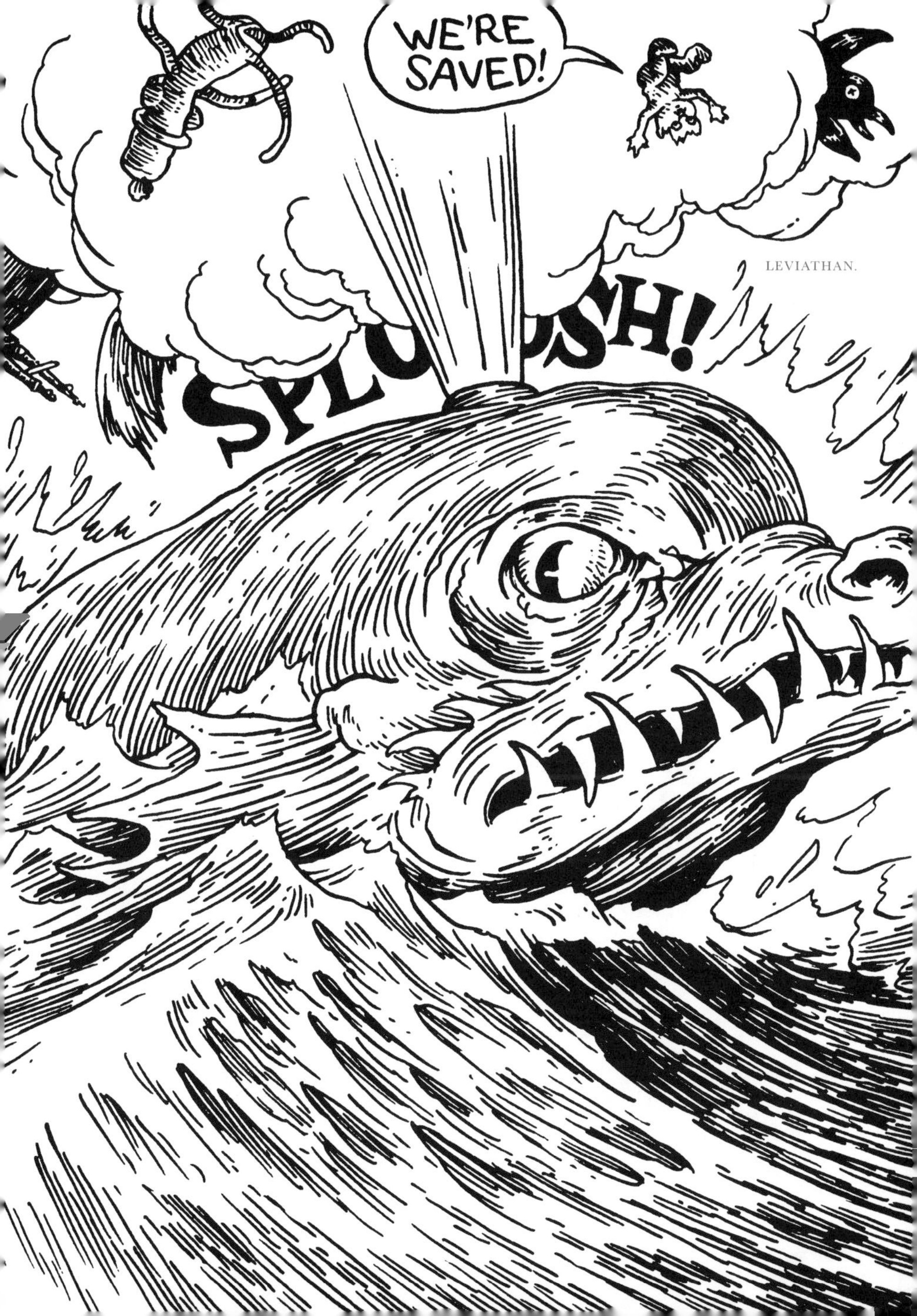
WE'RE SAVED!
LEVIATHAN.
SPLOOSH!

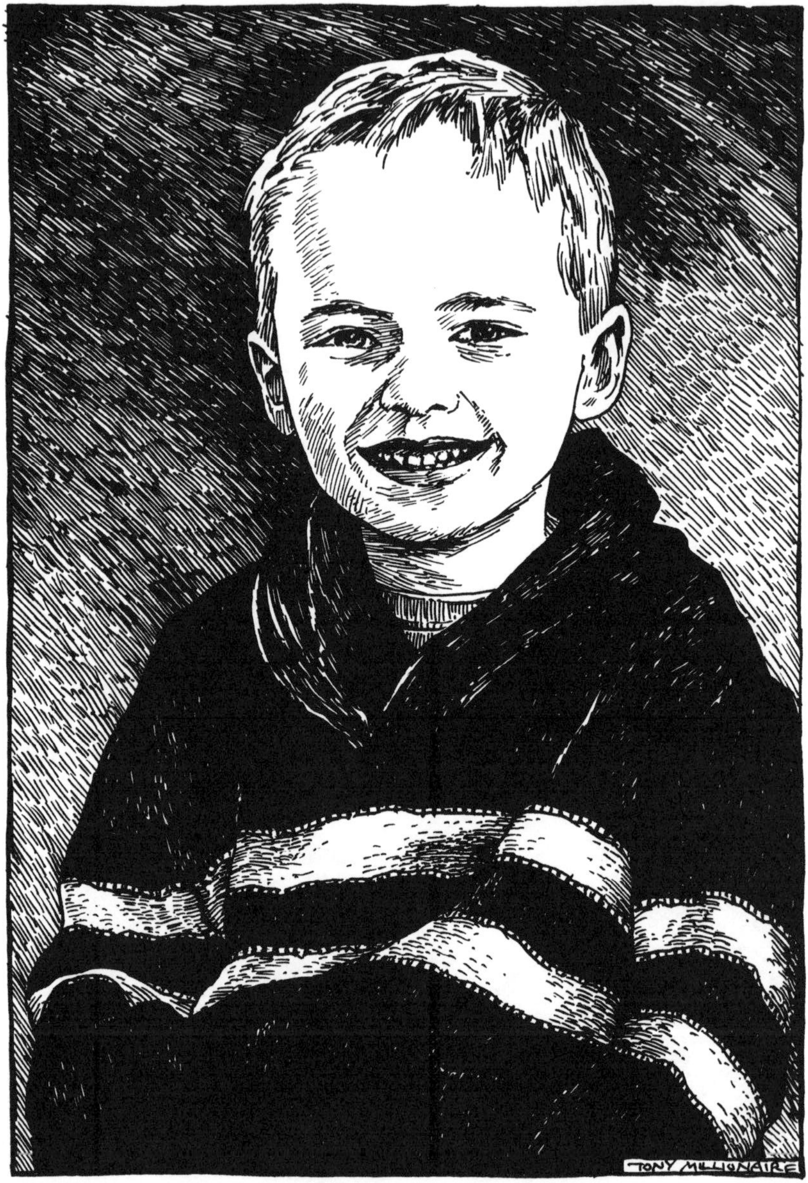
TONY MILLIONAIRE

CHARLIE CLOWES.

— S C H O O L S —

O n October 28th, 2000, I married Becky, and we quickly started pumping out children. Phoebe was born 10 months after our wedding. (I held my tiny baby in my arms, rocking her as I watched those buildings crumble on TV, thousands died and God knows how many copies of the *New York Press* with Drinky Crow in it were destroyed in that hellish scene.) And then, as if by magic, out popped Pearl two years later. We soon discovered that we had created the perfect family. Becky is a very talented comedic actress and I am a very talented comedic cartoonist, so it stands to reason that these two kids would be clever and funny. Well, now my 85% theory was all shot to hell when applied to small groups of people. Soon the girls were old enough to go to school and we found that a huge percentage of the kids in the schools were not bogus at all! The teachers were testing around 5% bogus, the kids had a few wise guys mixed in, bringing their bogus number up to about 3%, way out of whack with my regular numbers! Was it all just Happy Day Talk? Kids and teachers and the good life? I soon found out where the numbers were hidden! It was within the parents, the committees, and all the hangers-on. Here were large groups of people, double the number of students and teachers, and these knuckle-heads were completely skewing the numbers, but in a way that balanced out the school situation and solved the mystery. These parent types are easily 93% bogus!

PEARL MILLIONAIRE by PEARL

MRS. MILLIONAIRE and DAUGHTER PHOEBE, by PHOEBE

SUPERTEACHER.

MAD TEEN SCIENTIST.

TEEN TRAVEL REPORTER.

QUEEN AWESOME.

WHITNEY.

CAT.

PETER LANDAU.

JOHN HAWKES.

JOHN HODGMAN.

JOHN SELLERS.

JOHN HOWARD KUNSTLER.

JORGE LUIS BORGE.

CTHULU.

BOB ODENKIRK.

BENJAMIN WEISSMAN.

BRUCE JAY FRIEDMAN.

CHARLES S. JOHNSON.

CHRISTIAN HAWKEY.

CARLOS ROTELLA.

MILLICENT DILLON.

JANET MALCOLM.

JESSIE FAUSET.

JOAN SILBER.

THOMAS FRANK.

JIM KNIPFEL.

JULIA SLAVIN.

JARED PAUL STERN.

SARAH MANGUSO.

SCOTT BRADFIELD.

TAYARI JONES.

MARY WILLIAMS.

ZADIE SMITH.

WILLIAM KENNEDY.

LYDIA DAVIS.

W.E.B. DuBOIS.

ADAM McKAY.

ALAINE LeROY LOCKE.

CHARLES BAXTER.

ETGAR KERET.

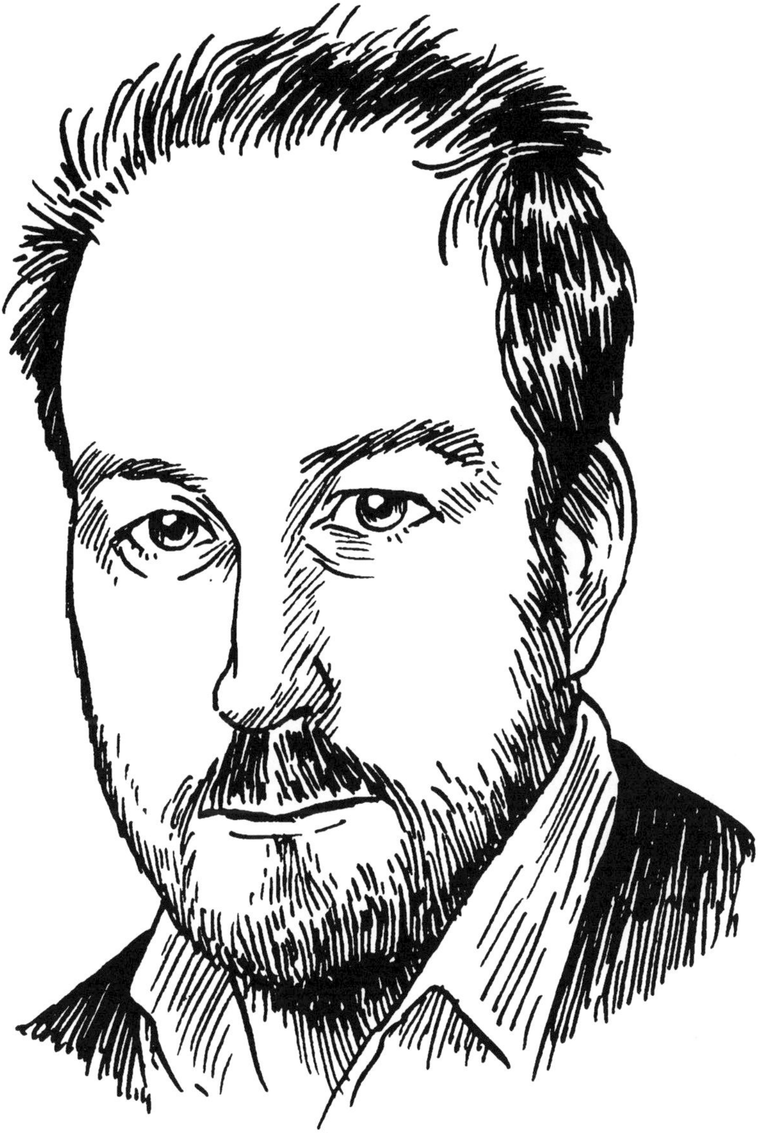

ANTHONY SWOFFORD.

ROCKPORT

My grandparents had a little gallery on the dock in Rockport, Mass. It had small glass-paned windows on three walls, with a beautiful view of the harbor and the Atlantic Ocean. My grandmother would generally paint portraits, she was a real master. Watercolor is a tough medium for portraits, because every mistake you make is very difficult to hide, unlike oil, which you can just paint out and do over. But Grammy was quick, if she made a mistake she would rub that paper with a tiny round natural sponge till it was raw and then paint over it. Her portraits had an inner glow from all that transparent water color. Grampop was quite good at drawing and illustration and he got cover jobs for *Open Road for Boys*, *Thrilling Western*, and *Action Stories*. ¶ Sundays at my Grammy and Grampop's house was nice. They lived in a very small house, which used to be the carriage house to the big house next door. There were paintings and drawings all over the walls, beautiful lamps, statuettes, and antiques. A tapestry hung from the loft. The place smelled wonderful, linseed oil, turpentine and Grampop's pipe tobacco! The Seth Thomas clock ticked all night. In the morning coffee and bacon were made. The kids

had pancakes. I watched my Grampop pull out his pen box and start to whittle pencils. There was lots of stuff in that wooden box, pens and pencils, sponges and gum erasers, hard white erasers and pots of ink. In one compartment there were lots of pen nibs, all jumbled in a pile. ¶ He would take a razor blade with a piece of tape on one side, and sharpen the pencil lead to a long fine point. He told me to use a hard 4H pencil if I was going to sketch for an ink drawing. He'd sketch out something, always drawing from life or from a sketch he had done out in the woods. Then I'd get bored and read the Sunday comics. Boston had two papers so we had lots to choose from. *Moon Mullins, Captain Easy, Blondie, Terry and the Pirates, Prince Valiant.* My grandfather loved all that old stuff, then I'd turn to *Peanuts,* my favorite. He didn't like *Peanuts,* he said it was kids' stuff, too simple. I remember once he took out a big leather portfolio of his collection of Sunday comics, and he laid it on the floor. He was friends with Roy Crane and Les Turner, he said in Art College they would always ask him to come over and have a drink with them. He thought maybe they wanted him to work with them on their comics, "But all they wanted was to hear mah Texas accent!" he would laugh.

MAREN & FREYA COVEY.

BIKER SANTA and ELF.

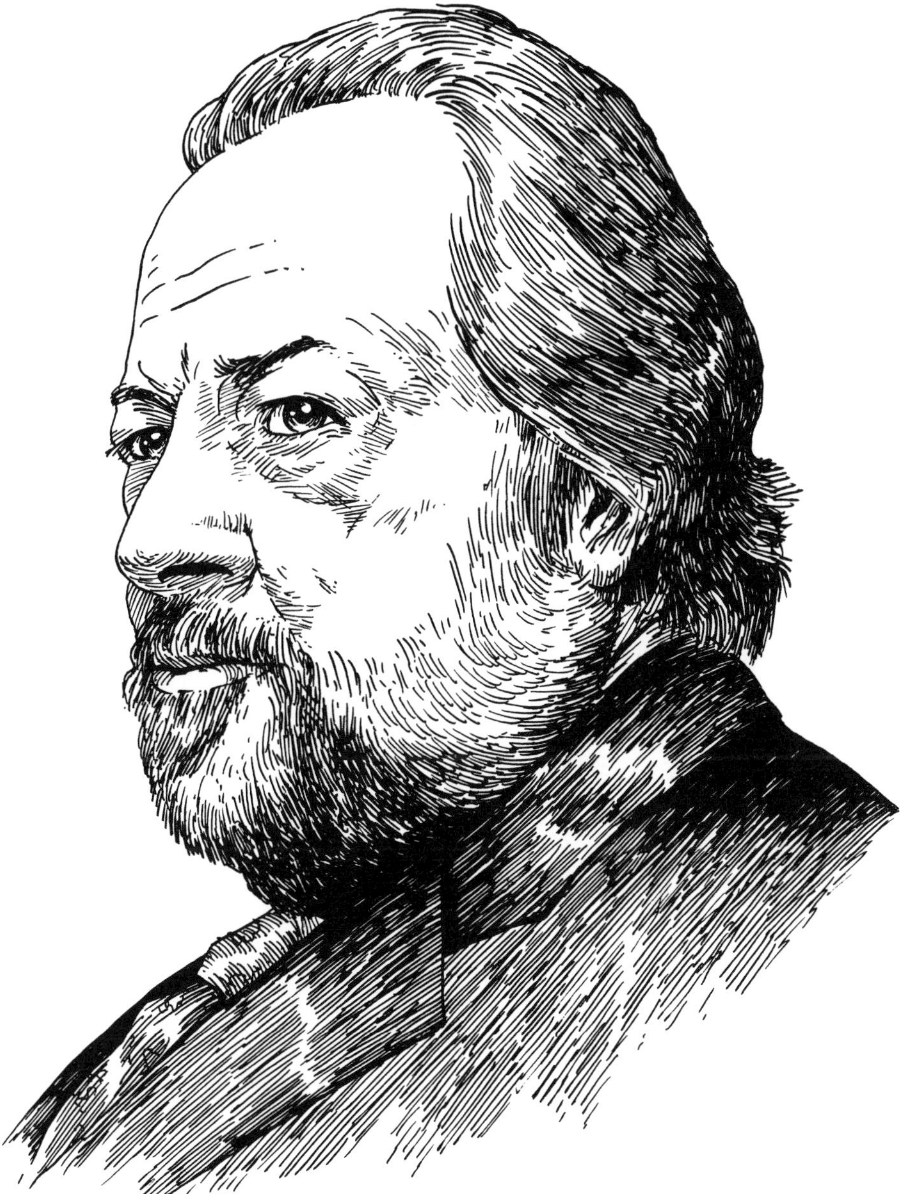

RICKY JAY.

KARL MARX.

DANIEL DENNET.

TOM DUMM.

SLAVOJ ŽIŽEK.

YODA.

SILVIA BENSO.

ARTURO SCHOMBERG.

LITERATE DOG.

JOHN WOLDEMAR COWAN.

JACQUES BAILLY.

JOEL STEIN.

JOHN WALTER SCOTT.

DARREN O'DONNELL.

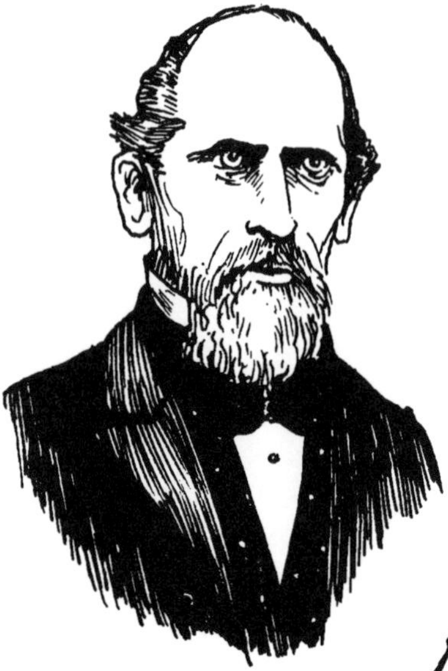

JOHN A. ROEBLING.

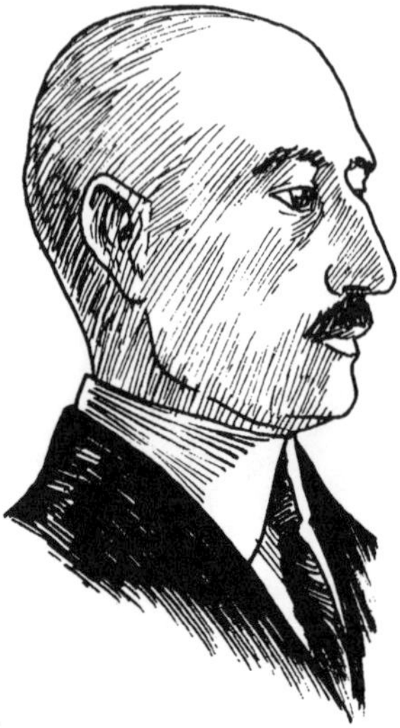

OLE SINGSTAD.

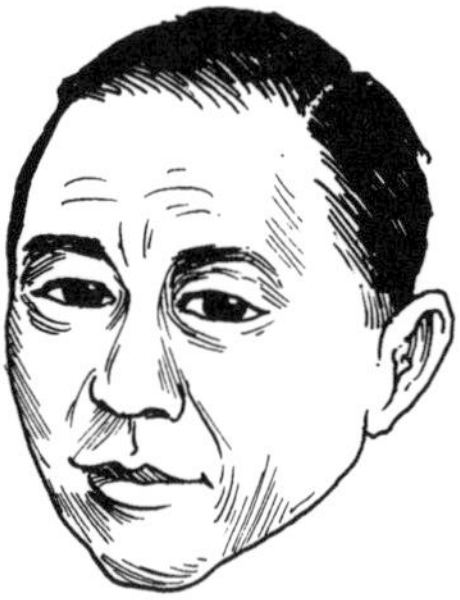

MINORU YAMASAKI.

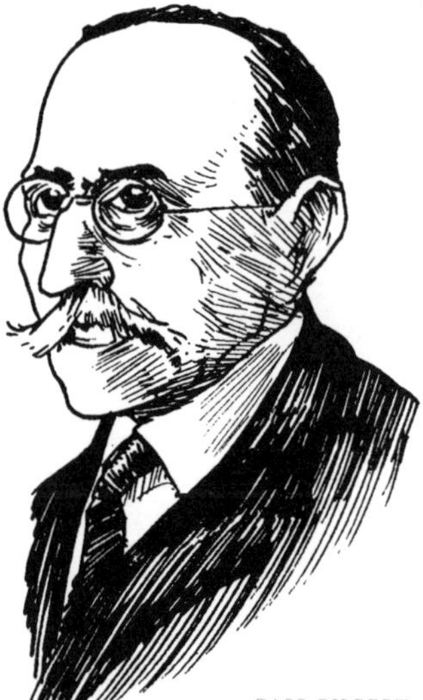

CASS GILBERT.

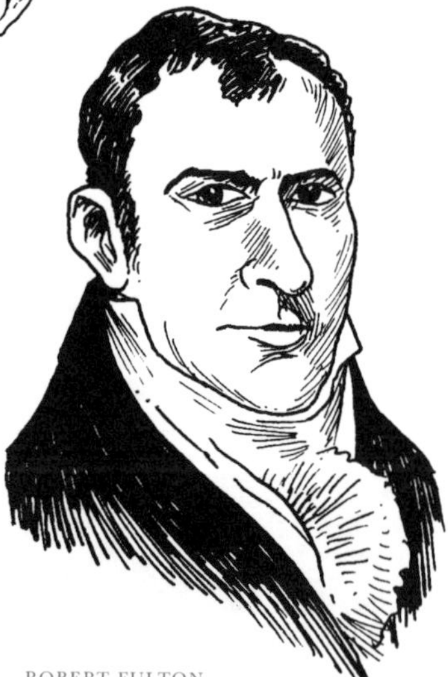

ROBERT FULTON.

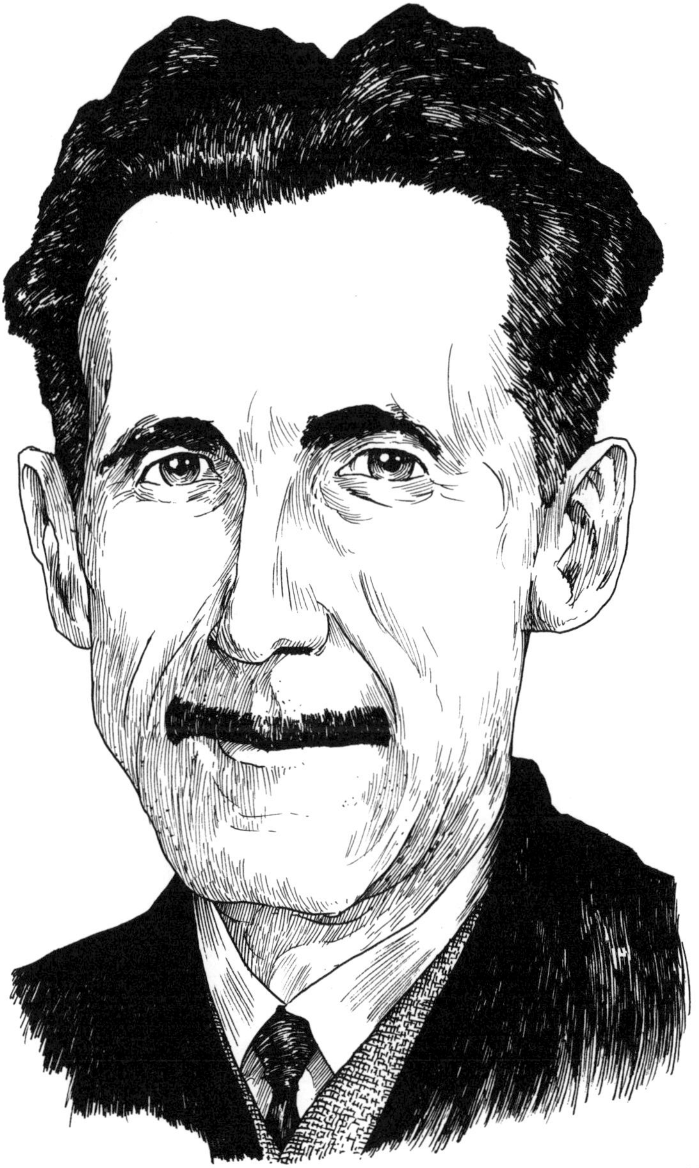

GEORGE ORWELL.

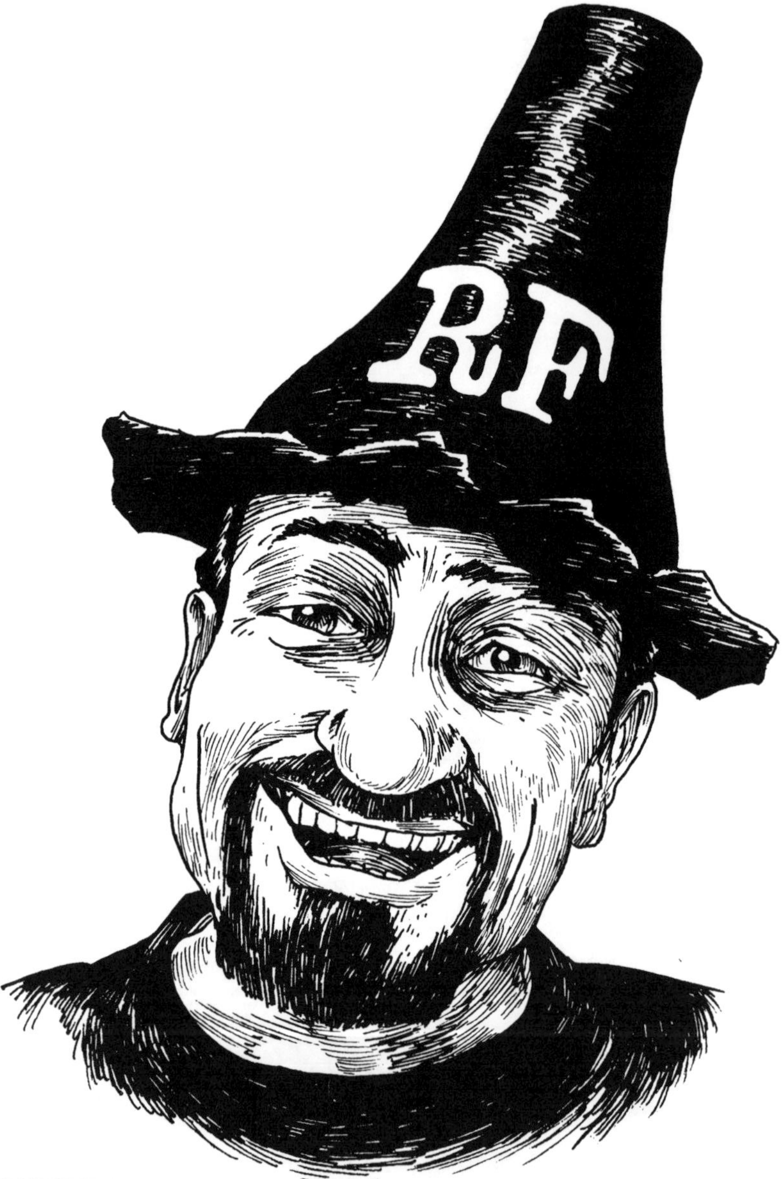
RF

ED "BIG DADDY" ROTH.

MATT VERTA and JON SPENCER.

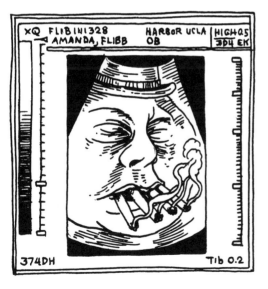

XAVIER MORA.

SOCK MONKEY and MR. CROW.

MICHÉLE ROTHEN.

THOMAS HELD.

DANIEL BINSWANGER.

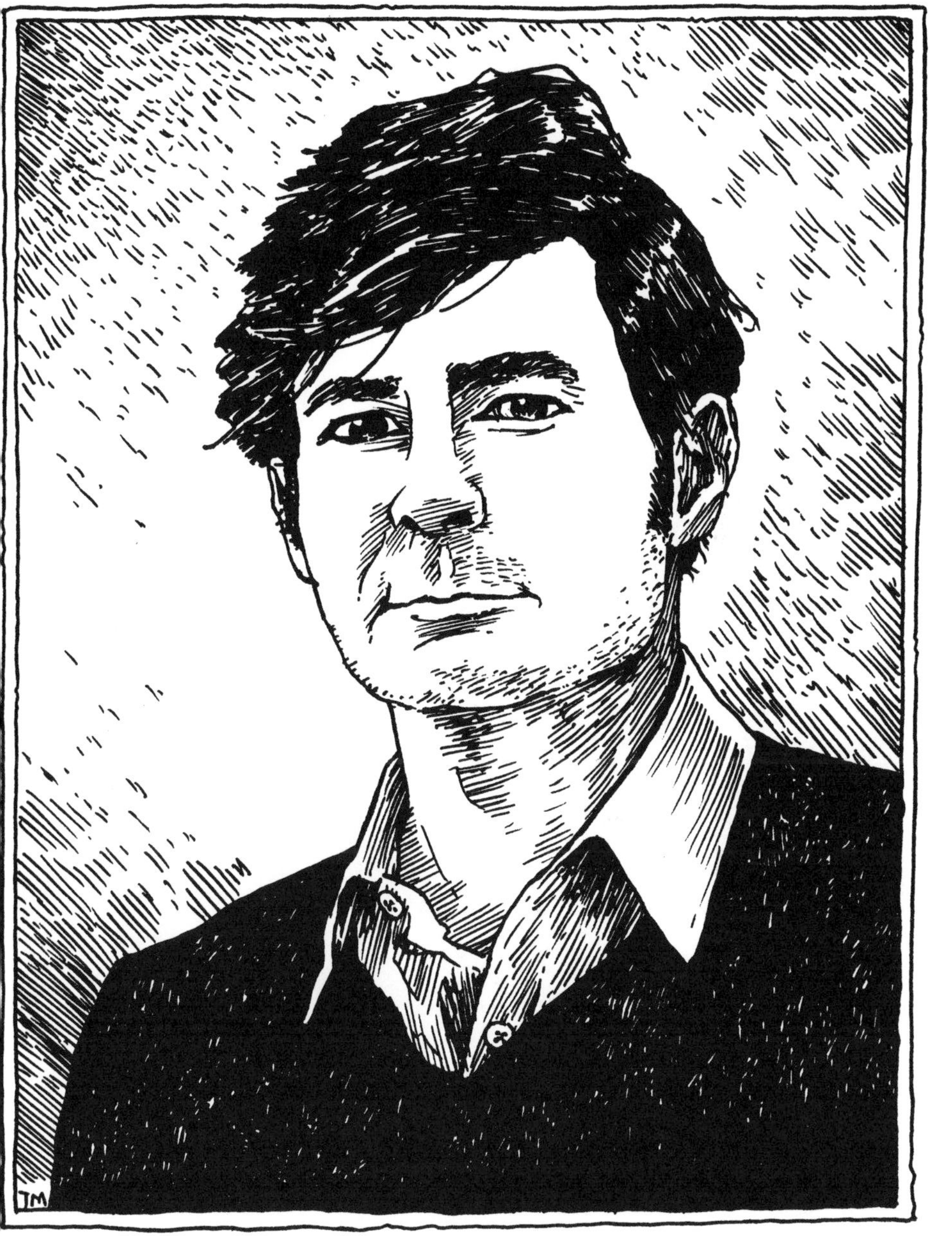
TM

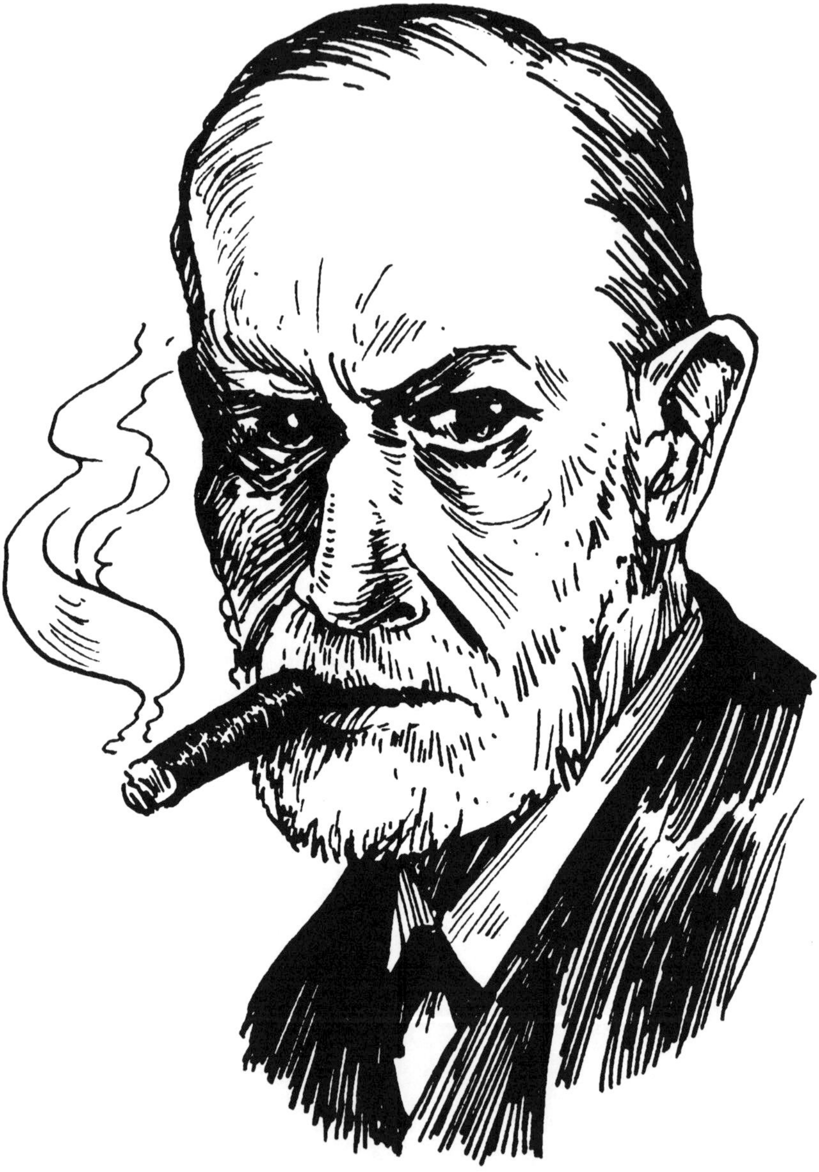

SIGMUND FREUD.

MOTHER

My grandfather gave me a great tip for drawing houses. I tended to fill in the windows black. He taught me to take a razor blade or an Exacto blade and scratch the black windows a little to give the impression of a reflection in the window, to make the drawing come alive. It does work, although I shouldn't use the word impression, he hated the impressionists and he hated "that bastard" Picasso even more. "Why, he admitted he was a phony on TV!" exclaimed he and my grandmother. They were both traditionally trained artists from the Pennsylvania Academy of Fine Arts in Philadelphia, and hated Modern Art. My mother taught me the trick, when drawing eyeballs, always put a couple of lines on the bottom of the whites, right on the whites. You'd think it would make the portrait googly-eyed, but it doesn't, it really works, when you remember to do it.

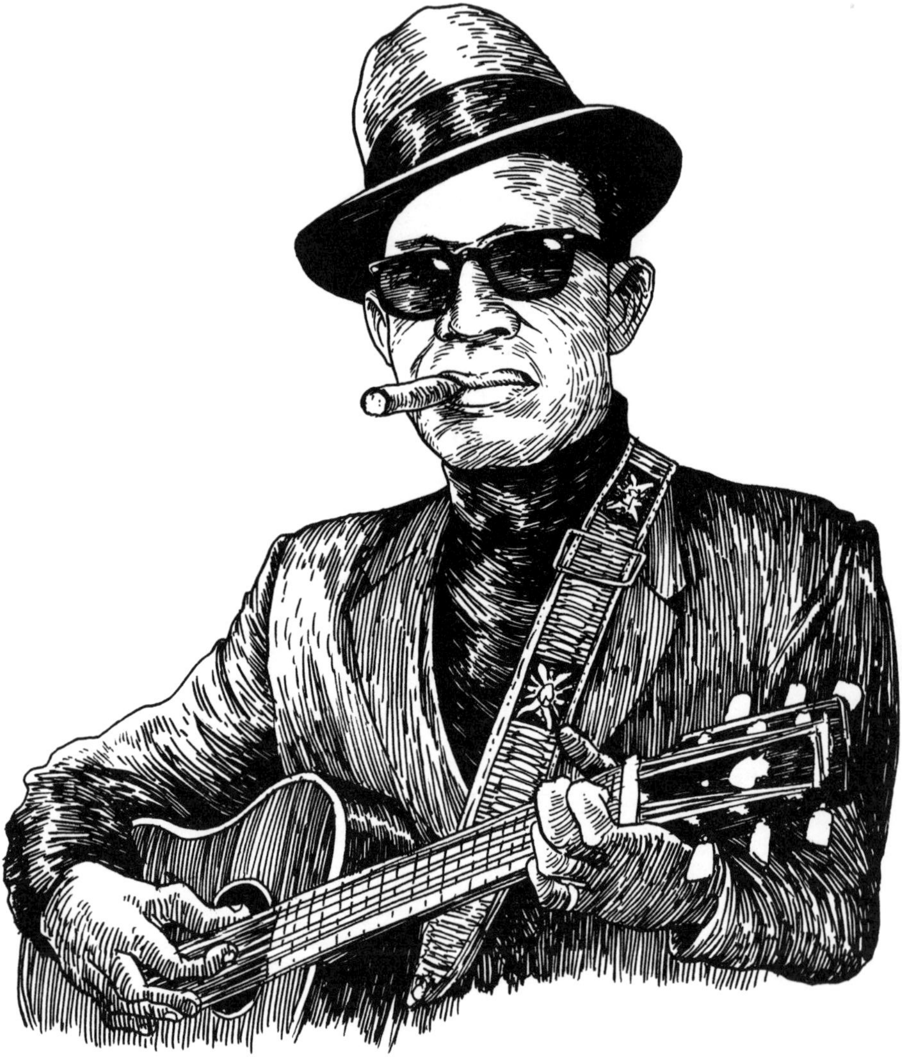

LIGHTNIN' HOPKINS.

JONATHAN HAIDT.

PHILIP G. ZIMBARDO.

PETER FITZPATRICK.

FREDERICK CULLEN.

ART GARFUNKEL.

PAUL SIMON.

SUSIE SUH.

DUKE ELLINGTON.

ROBERT FORSTER.

MICK JAGGER.

YO LA TENGO.

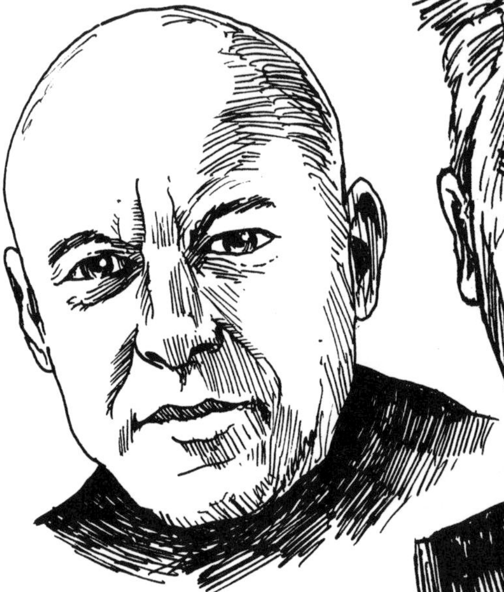

BRIAN ENO.

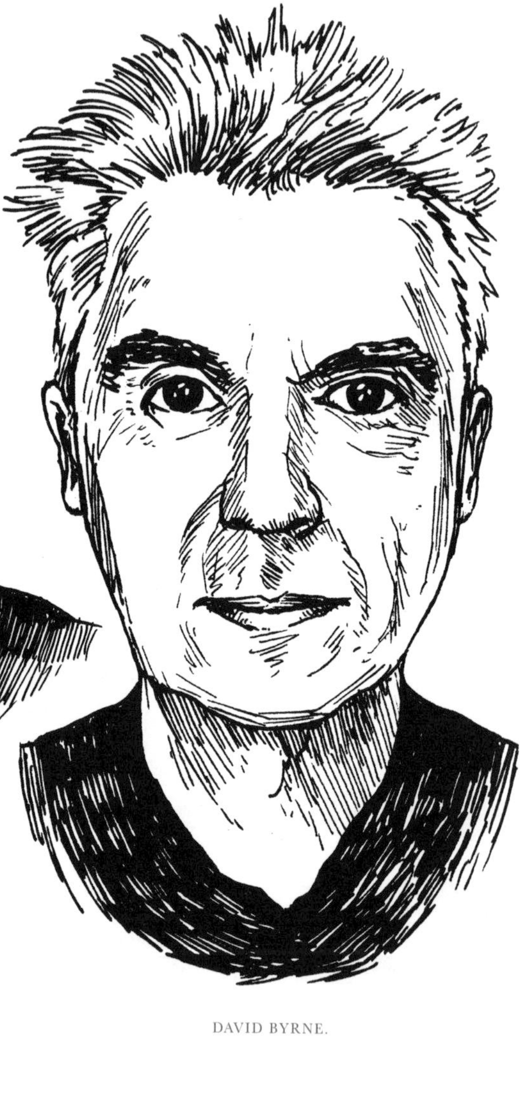

DAVID BYRNE.

MARTHA WAINWRIGHT.

JOHN RODERICK.

ROBYN HITCHCOCK.

NAT ADDERLEY.

SAMMY DAVIS, JR.

MILDRED BAILEY
and RED NORVO.

THE MILT JACKSON QUARTET.

DIZZY GILLESPIE.

EVA TAYLOR and CLARENCE WILLIAMS.

JUNIOR MANCE.

SADIE HARRIS FAGAN and BILLIE HOLIDAY.

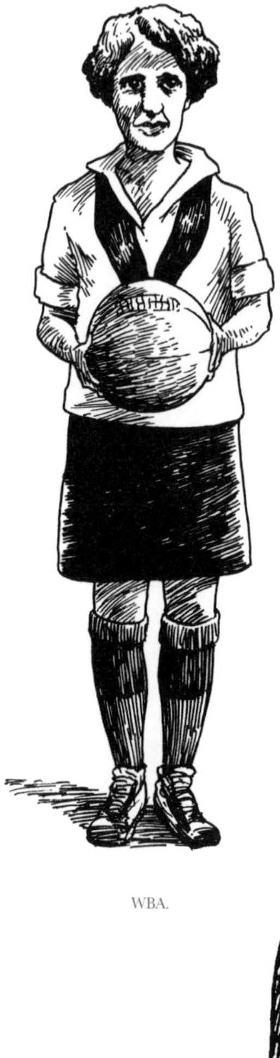

WBA.

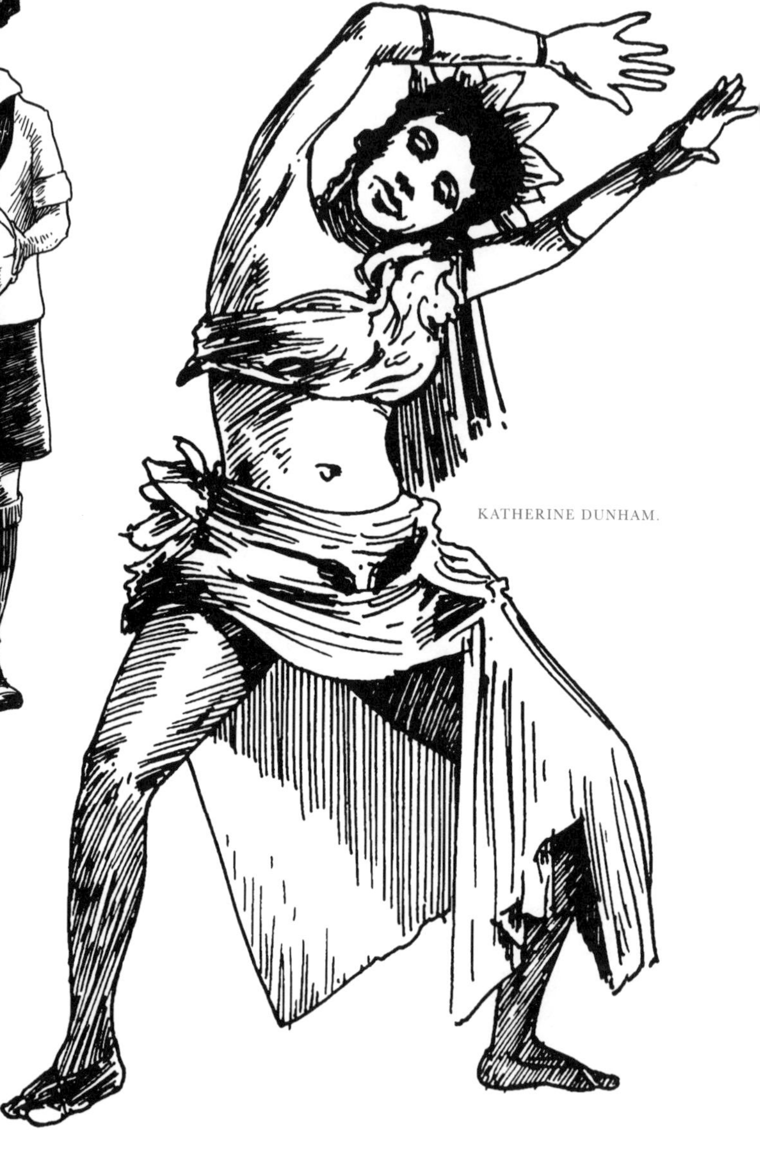

KATHERINE DUNHAM.

ALVIN AILEY.

ATHEA GIBSON.

HOWARD COSELL.

WNBA.

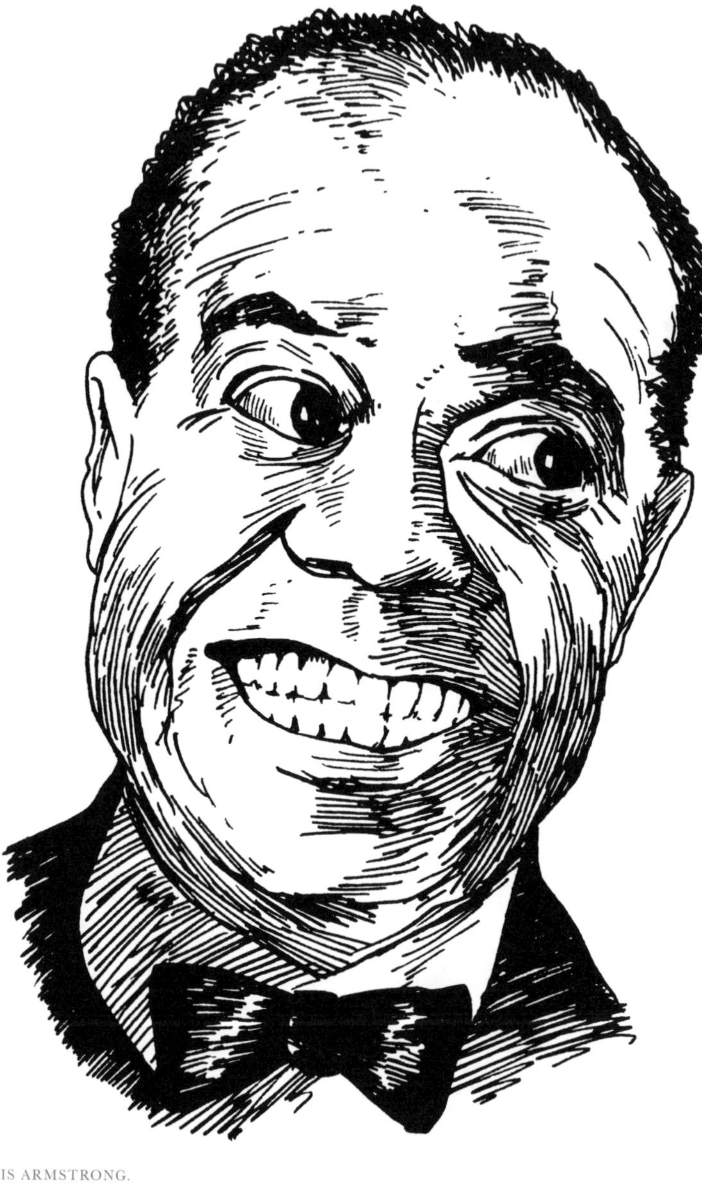

LOUIS ARMSTRONG.

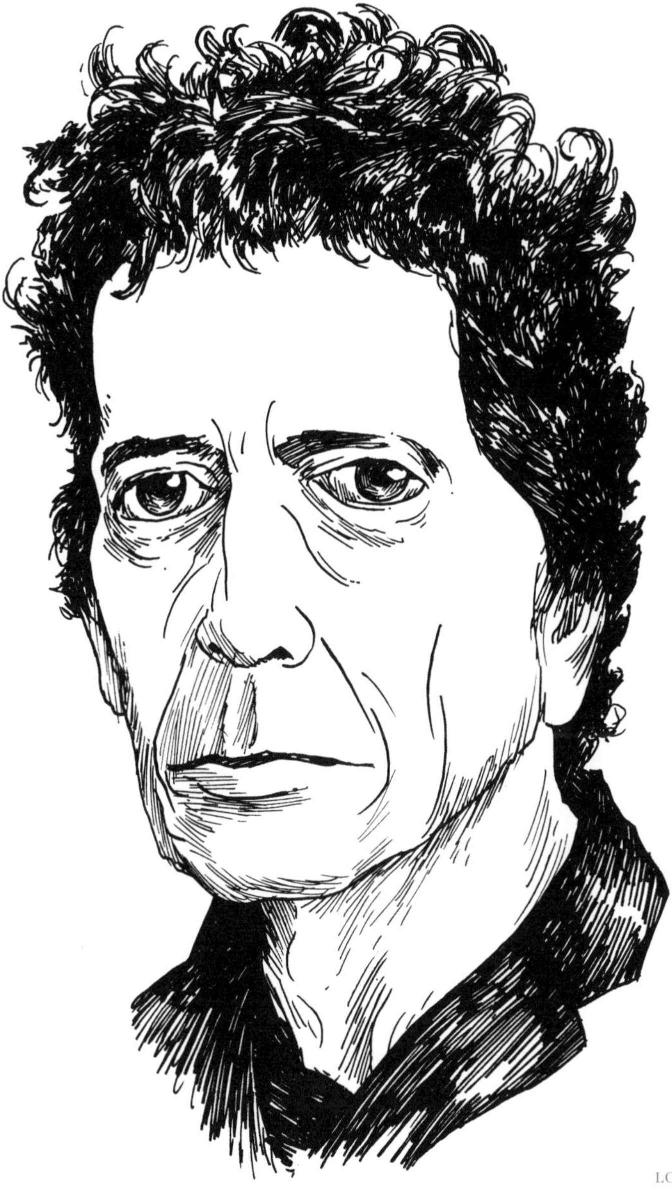

LOU REED.

BENNY GOODMAN.

TONY BENNETT.

PAT MARTINO.

TOM ZE.

TREY ANASTASIO.

MIKE DOUGHTY.

HEAVY TRASH.

WHEEL OF TIME.

FRENCHY.

AFRICAN WOMAN.

POPE JOHN PAUL II.

JOHN F. & JACQUELINE KENNEDY.

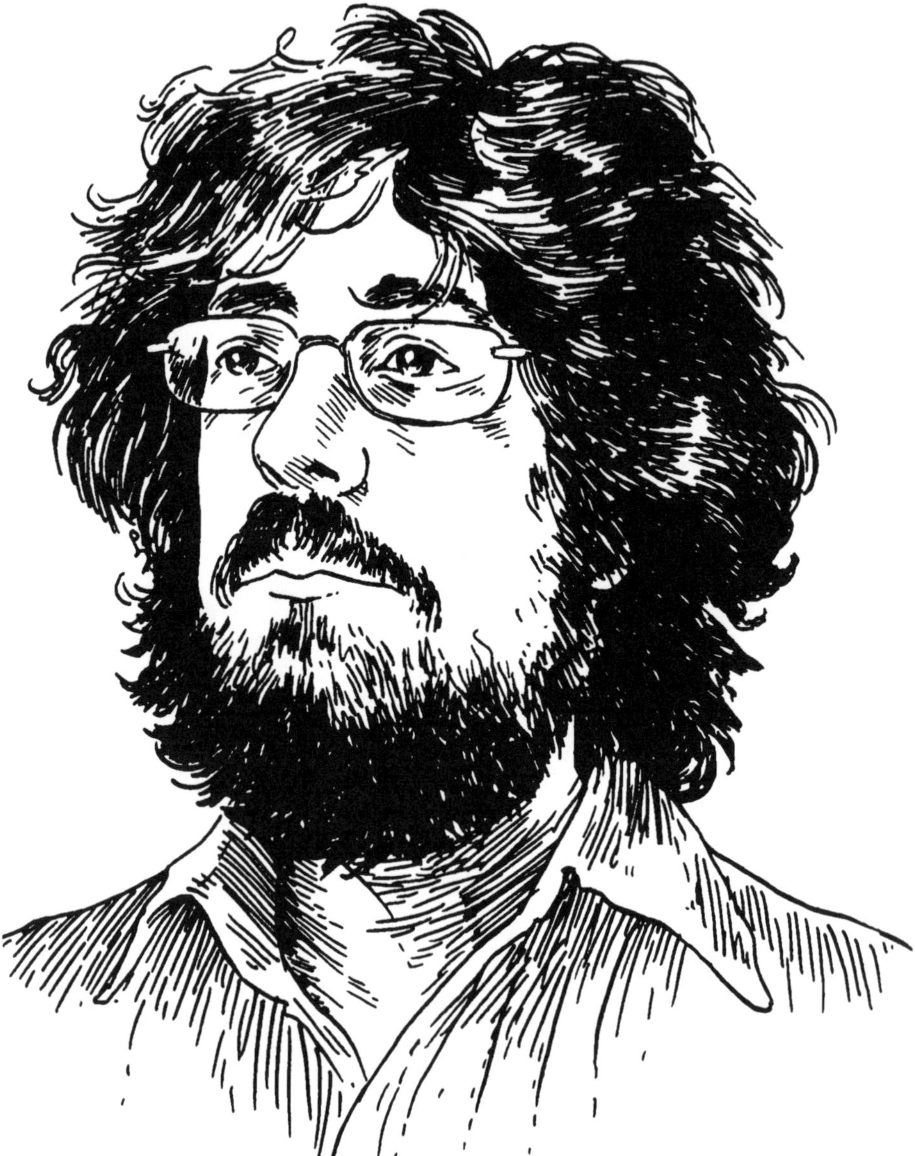

ERIC KAPLAN.

P H O T O G R A P H S

I want to talk about drawing from photographs. My Grammy told me once that she does not like to do it at all, but will if it's a commission or a portrait of a dead person. She told me to never draw from a photo until I had mastered drawing from life. You can almost always tell if a drawing came from a photo, not only is there a big goofy smile or expression which a sitter cannot hold for a real portrait, but most importantly, when drawing from life you can see the human connection, the full roundness of the face, the actuality of being there in front of the subject. It's hard to explain with puny words, sometimes you have to say things like "actuality" which I'm not sure is even a word, but the facts are the facts. Look at the portrait of The Human Lard Dog on page 59, the one with the LARD sign hanging around his neck. Or look at the portrait of Eric Kaplan (OPPOSITE) or Johnny Ryan on page 56 and you can see the difference. These portraits were all done in the room. After decades of practice I feel that I can get a decent drawing from a photo now, but there are some glaring examples in this book of my failures. ¶ When drawing from a photo I used to try to capture the shape of the head and then place the features within that egg-shaped skull bone. It doesn't work! It never works. I watched other portrait artists and did a little research and found that if I start with the eyes, place them properly so that the guy doesn't look cross-eyed right off the bat, that the rest would fall into place, and it does, most of the time. Techniques and tricks are different for everyone. I work from the eyes, try to keep the head big enough so I have enough room, but not so big that it turns into a giant uncontrollable mess. I like to work small, about seven inches high for a head.

LIZ COHEN.

RAYMOND PETTIBON.

DAVID HOCKNEY.

JACK GOLDSTEIN.

JOHN BALDESSARI.

GILBERT and JAIME HERNANDEZ.

JACOB LAWRENCE.

WILLIAM H. JOHNSON.

CHARLES ALSTON.

MONA LISA.

AUGUSTA SAVAGE.

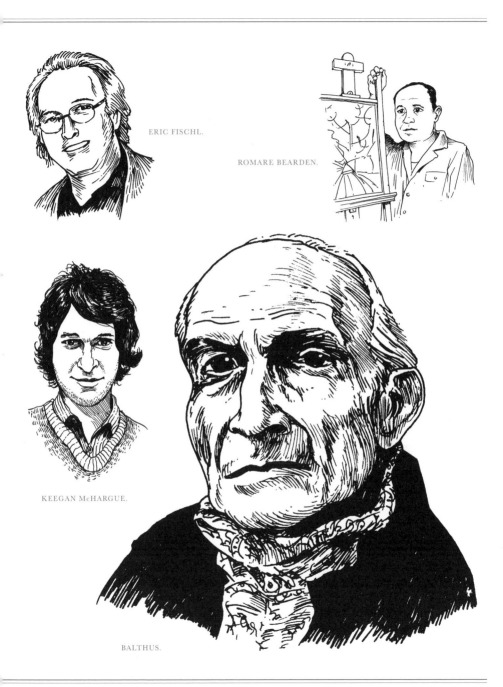

ERIC FISCHL.

ROMARE BEARDEN.

KEEGAN McHARGUE.

BALTHUS.

JOHN CROWLEY.

BARRY HANNAH.

DAVID MITCHELL.

LAWRENCE WESCHLER.

DEENAH VOLLMER.

MISHA GLOUBERMAN.

HAROLD McGHEE.

MICHAEL SILVERBLATT.

JAMES McMANUS.

JOSH FRUHLINGER.

DAVID THOMPSON.

LINDA THOMPSON.

MATT DANNER.

MIKE SMITH.

CHARLOTTE OSGOOD MASON.

GUSTAVO TURNER.

HELEN SIMPSON.

HEATHER CHAPLIN.

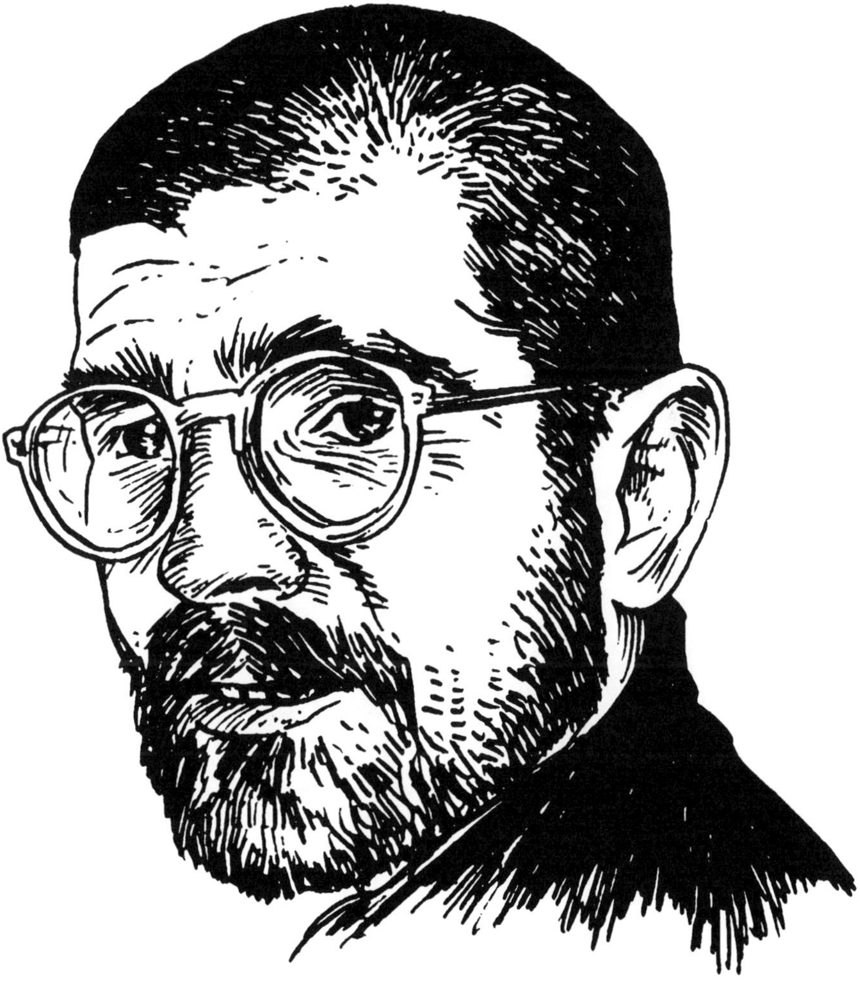

DAVID MAMET.

GARY FRANCIONE.

THURGOOD MARSHALL.

ALEXANDRA KORRY.

DUNG BEETLE.

DAVID BRAFF.

ERIC KRAUTHEIMER.

ALINE TREDE.

BASTIEN GIROD.

ANTONIO HODGERS.

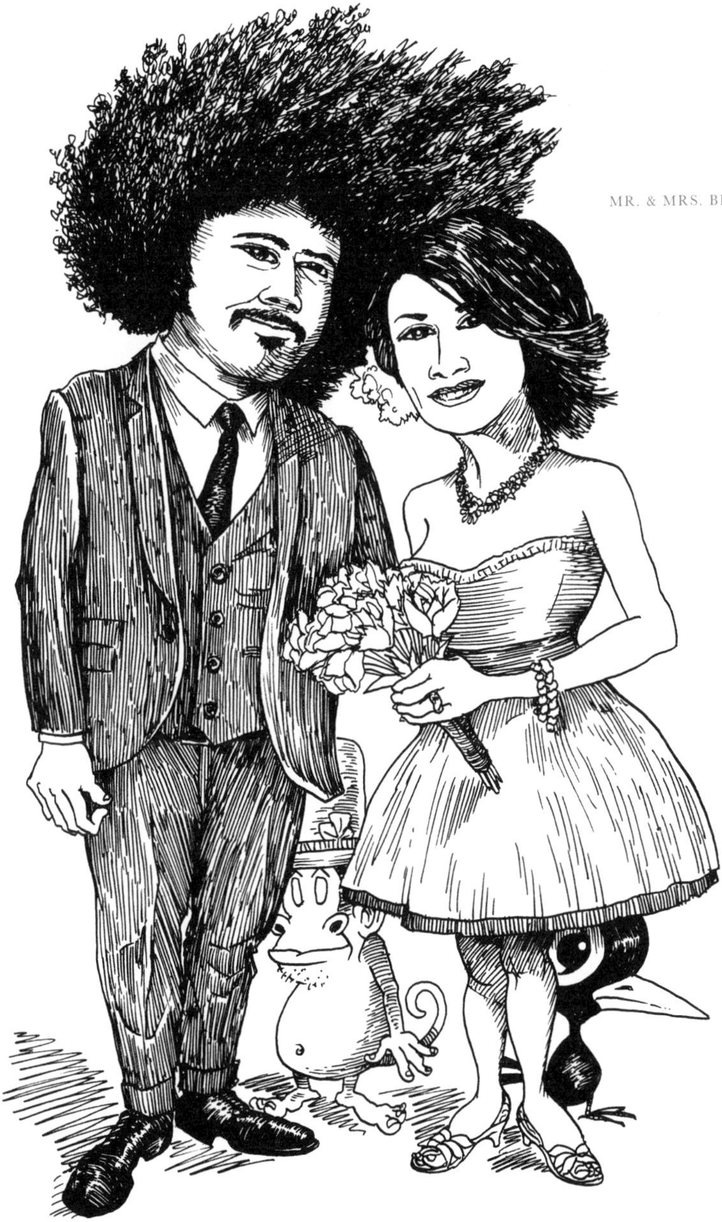

MR. & MRS. BLOOD.

WHAT I DO

kay, here's what I do: Sit down at the table, slanted up about 15 degrees. I like a hard wooden chair and a home-made table. I made it out of a narrow Victorian end table onto which I fastened a smooth piece of thick plywood, with supports at the back. I painted the whole thing with dark cherry-wood polyurethane stain. It's beautiful and functional, the perfect size with ball and claw feet. I put a small edge on the bottom and top so my pencils don't roll off. I put down a large piece of matt board, taped, which almost covers the beautiful cherry-wood plywood top. Smooth matt board, (not the textured kind) is the perfect drawing surface. I have two overhead lamps with 95 watt light bulbs, saving the environment from 10 watts of energy. I always use two because one leaves a big shadow of loneliness across the board. Grampop's advice, always keep the pencil sharp. I keep an electric pencil sharpener at the top of the table and use it every thirty seconds, the 4H must always be sharp. Hands must be super clean, any sweat or french fry grease ruins the drawing experience, so I wash my hands compulsively, every 15 minutes. I always cut an oval of the same bristol board I'm drawing on, about 4x3 inches, to rest my hand on. This sticks to my hand and I slide it back and forth over the blank paper so that it gets smooth enough to glide and the heel of my hand can grip it. This prevents the enemy of paper, hand sweat, from ever getting on the paper. The worst would be dragging ink across the paper, which I have done.
¶ After I get a good drawing down I have to work on cleanup. Sometimes that means massive skull and facial surgery in Photoshop, but

[CONT'D] sometimes not. The originals can often be sold or given as gifts especially if the person is famous and can give you a job or introduce you to someone with a giant pile of golden money. So it's important to try and save the original. White paint has been used for centuries. I don't like it. I've seen it on old originals, on old comics pages which were normally thrown out after they were printed. The white paint and Wite-Out always sticks out and has a different color. I hate the use of blue pencils too, people use them because it doesn't show up in print, but what a mess! ¶ Here's what I do, my father taught me this trick. He's a designer. I always draw on heavy 3-ply bristol board. I take a sharp Exacto blade and cut around and carefully peel off what I don't want. It works for small areas, but not for large spots. Then I take a scrap of bristol and lay it over the wound. Rub it hard with the back of the Exacto knife handle, you douchebags, rub and rub, and you will get a fine clean flat burnished spot, which you can draw over if you're careful. As for ink and pens, forget it, you're on your own. I use pens and inks that are not waterproof and I would not recommend them, so ask an expert.

Tony Millionaire uses the Rotring ArtPen (EF) but does not use the weak gray ink cartridges that come with the pen, nor the gray soup they sell in boxes at American art supply stores. He buys his cartridges exclusively from dealers on eBay. This is the good black stuff from Germany. It is still not waterproof but it is true black. —Ed. Note

INDEX TO PORTRAITS

[C O N T ' D]

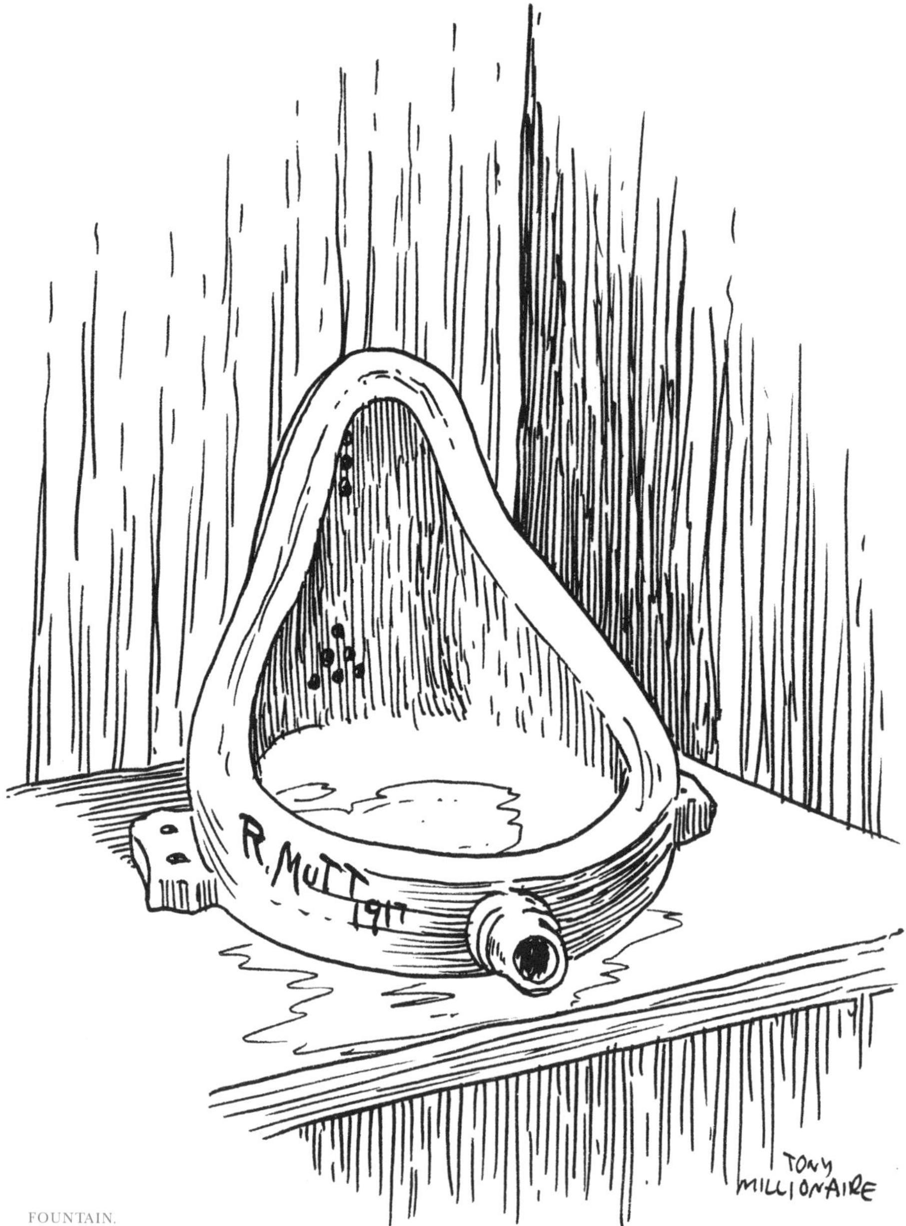
R. MUTT 1917
TONY
MILLIONAIRE

FOUNTAIN.

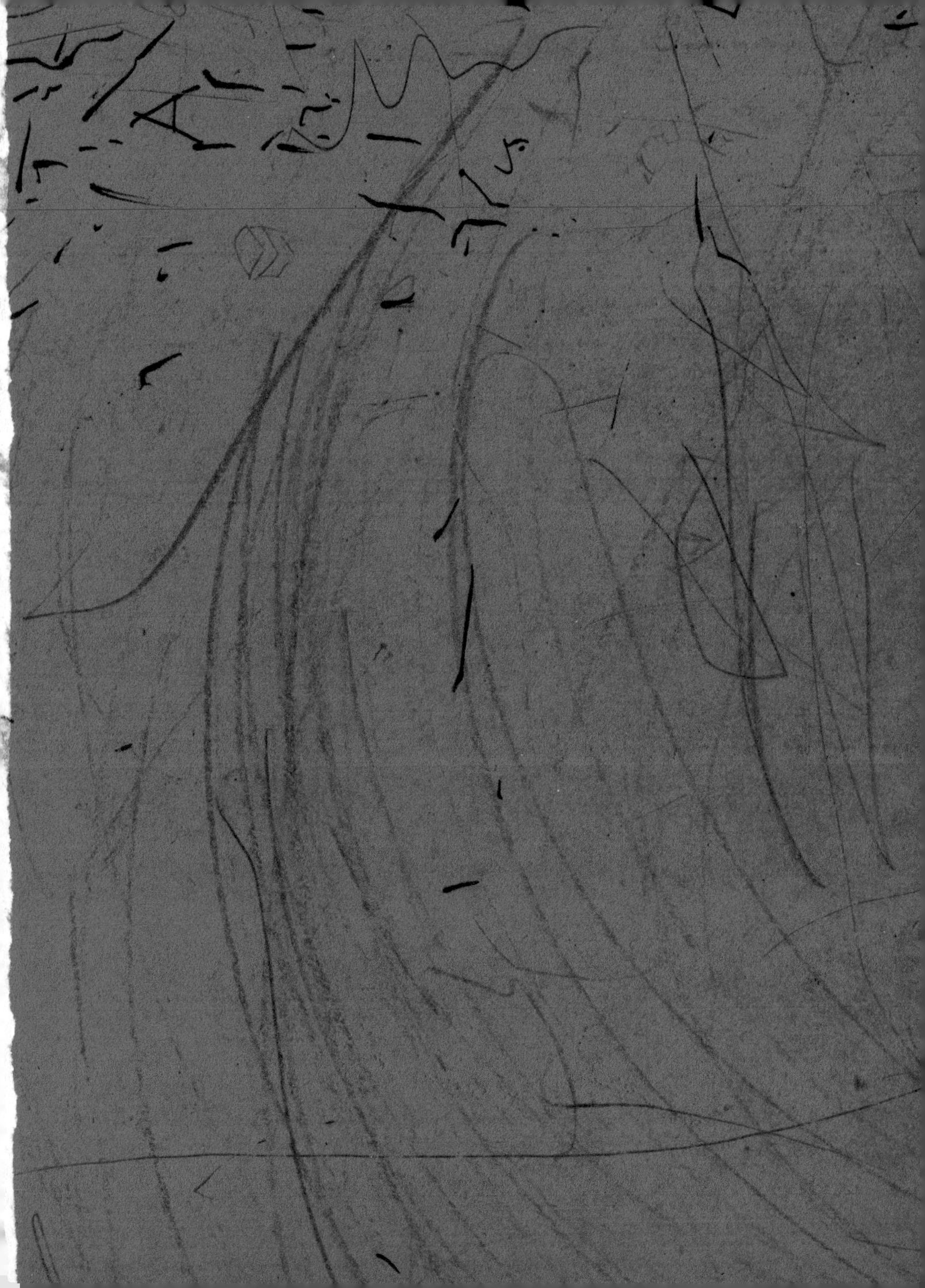